Puzzles about Human Rights

Puzzles about Human Rights

TIMOTHY EVES

Copyright © 2019 by Soft Skills Power, LLC

All rights reserved.
Published in the United States by Soft Skills Power, LLC.

ISBN: 978-1-951366-06-3

Cover design by Soft Skills Power, LLC

Soft Skills Power, LLC.
450 Lexington Avenue, #1479, New York, NY 10163
www.softskillspower.com

Printed in the United States of America

Table of Contents

PART I – Theories of Human Rights — 1
Puzzle 1: Bad Blood — 2
Puzzle 2: The Child in the Basement — 7
Puzzle 3: Noble Lie — 11
Puzzle 4: Theme and Variations — 14
Puzzle 5: Price Gouging — 18
Puzzle 6: The State of Nature — 23
Puzzle 7: Veil of Ignorance — 28
Puzzle 8: Abduction, Rape, and Forced Marriage — 34

PART II – The Rights to Life, Liberty, and Property — 39
Puzzle 9: Lifeboat — 40
Puzzle 10: Terri Schiavo — 44
Puzzle 11: A Tale of Two Cities — 50
Puzzle 12: "You Are Causing Aggression to Us" — 56
Puzzle 13: Desecration of the Flag — 65
Puzzle 14: Academic Freedom — 70
Puzzle 15: Legalization of Drugs — 79
Puzzle 16: Extreme Poverty — 83

PART III – Who Has Rights — 88
Puzzle 17: *Roe v. Wade* — 89
Puzzle 18: Gay Marriage — 93
Puzzle 19: Mr. Data — 99
Puzzle 20: The Cave — 106

PART IV – Responding to Violations of Human Rights — 116
Puzzle 21: Home Invasion — 117
Puzzle 22: Disobedience, Civil and Otherwise — 122
Puzzle 23: The Ticking Bomb Case — 127

Sources and Further Reading — 130

PART I
Theories of Human Rights

Puzzle 1
Bad Blood

On May 16, 1997, in a White House ceremony, President Bill Clinton issued a formal apology on behalf of the nation. "What the United States did was shameful," he said, "and I am sorry." The apology was for violating the rights, over a period of four decades, of 399 African-American men who suffered from syphilis. By the time Clinton apologized, only a handful of them were still alive.

The events that culminated in Clinton's apology began in 1930, when the United States Public Health Service (PHS) launched a program in Macon County, Alabama, to diagnose and treat 10,000 African Americans for syphilis. The program, though well intentioned, proved overly ambitious. Testing revealed that 35% of African Americans living in Macon County were infected with the disease, a much higher percentage than was anticipated, so that treating everyone would have been a daunting task even with proper funding. But with the Great Depression underway, funding for programs like this was scarce. By 1931, the money for the program ran out. Only 1,400 people received even partial treatment.

Unable to treat any more patients, the PHS settled for conducting a six-month observational study, the cost of which was minimal. Working with the Tuskegee Institute, and getting assistance from black churches and community leaders, the PHS recruited participants for the study. The goal of the study was to determine the effects of untreated syphilis on African-American men. At the time, nobody knew very well what these effects were. Many believed – incorrectly, we now know – that syphilis had lesser effects on black Americans than on white Americans. If the observational study could yield more accurate knowledge of the effects of syphilis, physicians might be able – when funding once again became available – to provide more appropriate treatment. The study eventually came to involve 600 participants, 399 of whom had syphilis. The remaining 201 participants served as a control group.

The 399 men with syphilis, living in an impoverished part of the country and having little income and little education, knew next to nothing about health care. They knew from their symptoms that something was wrong with their health, but they didn't know what condition they had. Instead of informing them that they had syphilis, those conducting the study told them they had "bad blood." The participants were also told that they were receiving effective treatment when in fact they were given placebos. According to the PHS, "bad blood" was the term African Americans living in Macon County used for syphilis, but this was misleading. In reality, it was a catchall phrase that covered many conditions, including syphilis, but also including, for example, iron deficiency, sickle-cell disease, leukemia, and low energy. Thus, although the participants in the study all consented to their participation, their consent was less than fully informed.

At the end of the six months, the PHS learned that syphilis was just as deadly among black Americans as it was among white Americans. Hoping to learn more, the PHS extended the study – and kept on extending it, year after year after year.

In 1938, six years into the study, the United States passed the National Venereal Disease Control Act, which required the PHS to treat people suffering from syphilis. The PHS, however, chose not to treat the 399 men, on the grounds that, as participants in a scientific study, they weren't subject to the requirements of the law.

In 1947, fifteen years into the study, the Nuremberg Code was formulated. A response to the discovery of atrocities committed by Nazi experimenters, the Nuremberg Code set forth the basic rights that participants in scientific studies should be accorded. According to the Nuremberg Code, for a scientific study to be ethically justified, all human subjects must give their consent, their consent must be fully free, and their consent must be fully informed. Although the Tuskegee syphilis study clearly violated the Nuremberg Code, given that the participants weren't fully informed, the PHS allowed the study to continue.

In 1969, thirty-seven years into the study, the Centers for Disease Control (CDC) convened a panel to review the study. With only one dissenting member, the panel recommended that the study continue, arguing that treatment at such a late stage might cause more harm than good.

In 1972, forty years into the study, Jean Heller, a reporter for the Associated Press, discovering how the participants of the study were being treated, published her findings. The ensuing national outrage was what finally put an end to the study. By that time, twenty-eight of the participants had died from syphilis, another hundred had died from related complications, forty spouses had been infected, and nineteen children had been born with the disease.

Today, as in 1972, Americans are outraged when they learn about the Tuskegee syphilis study. For us today, the puzzle isn't whether the study was or wasn't morally justified. We overwhelmingly agree that it wasn't, and we might suspect that such an egregious violation of human rights could have happened only in a deeply racist society, that nothing of the sort would have happened had the participants been white instead of black. Still, the Tuskegee syphilis study raises a number of enormously difficult – and fundamental – questions about human rights. Here are a few of them.

1) What are human rights? Human rights advocates think of human rights as trump – they take precedence over other things that people value. If, for example, I have a right to life, you may not kill me, even if thousands of people hate my guts, so that my death would bring them great joy. Similarly, if I have a right to property, you may not steal my life savings, even if you donate the money to a charitable organization and the charitable organization uses the money to save thousands of lives. When the PHS conducted its study, it was with the hope of acquiring knowledge about the effects of syphilis, knowledge that could be used to save lives. Saving lives has great value. But what the PHS failed to recognize was that the rights of the participants in the study – as well as the rights of their families – should have taken precedence. We mustn't sacrifice the rights of a few hundred, or even one, to save the lives of thousands or millions. That, according to human rights advocates, is how powerful rights are.

But why should this be? Why should the rights of an individual trump the well-being of a society? Why isn't it the other way around, the well-being of a society trumping the rights of an individual? Because a society is larger than an individual, isn't it more valuable? Indeed, some philosophers, maintaining that societal well-being takes precedence over the individual, reject the notion of human rights. Jeremy Bentham (1748-1832), for example, famously derided human rights as "nonsense upon stilts" – although the notion appears elevated and noble, it's ultimately groundless, he thought.

2) Who has human rights? The answer to this question would seem to be obvious – those who have human rights are human beings. As human beings, the participants in the Tuskegee syphilis study had rights. The color of their skin didn't matter. Neither did their poverty or lack of education. Only their humanity mattered. By treating them as little more than laboratory animals, by acting as if they were less than fully human, the PHS violated their rights.

But why should humanity matter? Humanity is simply the biological fact of being a member of the species *Homo sapiens*. But why should this biological fact – but not skin color, which is also a biological fact – be relevant to having rights? If skin color, gender, eye color, the number of bones in one's hand, and other biological facts don't endow someone with rights, why should humanity? Perhaps, we might think, humanity matters because only human beings are able to understand rights, and it's this ability that gives human beings rights. Or perhaps humanity matters because only human beings are highly intelligent, or use language, or develop cultures. But none of this can be right, for the simple reason that some human beings – newborn babies and the very severely brain-damaged, for example – don't understand rights, aren't highly intelligent, don't use language, and don't develop cultures. Yet they, it seems, should be accorded rights just like any other human being. What feature or features, then, did the participants in the Tuskegee syphilis study have that endowed them with rights?

3) What rights do human beings have? Different writers provide different lists of rights. Take, for example, these four lists:

- John Locke (1632-1704): life, liberty, and property
- The Declaration of Independence (1776): life, liberty, and the pursuit of happiness
- The Universal Declaration of Human Rights (1948): life, liberty, and security of the person
- Tom Regan (1938-2017): life, liberty, and bodily integrity

One of the rights common to all four lists is the right to life. We might think this was the right that the PHS violated since so many of the syphilitic men died when they could have been saved. But what does it mean to have a right to life? On one plausible interpretation, a right to life is nothing more than a right not to be killed. But if this is what a right to life is, the PHS didn't violate anyone's right to life – they allowed a number of people to die, to be sure, but they didn't kill anybody. It was syphilis, not the PHS, that killed the participants in the study. Allowing to die might be a bad thing, maybe, as some philosophers believe, as bad as killing, but it's not the same thing as killing.

But perhaps a right to life means something else. Perhaps it means a right to be given the minimum one needs to survive. If this is right, the PHS violated the syphilitic men's right to life, because it failed to give these men the treatment they needed to continue living. The problem, though, is that this conception of a right to life is highly controversial. It implies, for example, that the sick have a right to receive health care, whether they can afford it or not. Although the National Venereal Disease Control Act of 1938, which required the PHS to treat people suffering from syphilis, is consistent with such a right, such a right would require the government – that is, taxpayers – to pay for the healthcare of the poor. Yet taxpayers have rights too, and requiring them to spend their hard-earned money on the health care of those whose illness they didn't cause seems to be a violation of their rights.

The upshot of all this is that, while the Tuskegee syphilis study seems clearly wrong, exactly what makes it wrong is difficult to pin down.

> *Questions for reflection: What makes the Tuskegee syphilis study morally wrong? Did the PHS violate anyone's right to life? What are human rights? Who has human rights? Which rights do human beings have?*

Puzzle 2
The Child in the Basement

"With a clamor of bells that set the swallows soaring, the Festival of Summer came to the city Omelas, bright-towered by the sea." With these words, Ursula K. Le Guin begins "The Ones Who Walk Away from Omelas," a short story about the high price of happiness.

To celebrate the Festival of Summer, processions of the people of Omelas head to the Green Fields in the northern part of town, where a much anticipated horse race is scheduled to take place. As they arrive, they enjoy food from the provisioners' tents – children's faces are "amiably sticky" and an old man's gray beard traps "a couple of crumbs of rich pastry." Young men wear "flowers in their shining hair," and passersby pause to listen to a boy, about ten years old, play a flute, "his dark eyes wholly rapt in the sweet, thin magic of the tune." As the riders, all boys and girls, lead their horses to the starting line, "the horses rear on their slender legs." Excitement is in the air. Everyone is happy.

The happiness, however, has little to do with the Festival of Summer. The people of Omelas were happy before the festival began, and they'll be happy after it ends. They're always happy. What kind of city is Omelas that could generate unending happiness? Le Guin shares some of the happiness-producing customs that Omelas embraces as well as some of the unhappiness-producing customs that it eschews. For the most part, though, she leaves it up to her readers to imagine Omelas as they like: "Perhaps it would be best if you imagined it as your own fancy bids, assuming it will rise to the occasion, for certainly I cannot suit you all." Thus, Omelas eschews clergy but embraces religion, Le Guin leaving unspecified what religion or religions the people of Omelas practice. Again, Omelas eschews automobiles and helicopters but embraces other technologies, Le Guin leaving unspecified which technologies it embraces: it might have "central heating, subway trains, washing machines, and all kinds of marvelous devices not yet invented here," or it might "have none of that; it doesn't matter." For less puritanical readers, Omelas might permit orgies or *drooz*, a non-habit-forming drug that reveals the "inmost secrets of the Universe" and heightens "the pleasure of sex beyond belief." Yet if the people of Omelas are already happy, "I really don't think many of them need to take *drooz*."

Omelas appears to be a wonderful city in which to live. But if it seems too good to be true, that's because it is. As it turns out, not quite everyone in Omelas is happy. Somewhere in the city is a basement, and somewhere in the basement is a tiny dark room, "about three paces long and two wide." Locked inside the room are an old bucket and two mops "with stiff, clotted, foul-smelling heads." Also locked inside the room is a child. The child might be a boy, or it might be a girl. Like the boy who plays the flute, this child is about ten years old – although it looks more like six. It is terrified of the mops, closing its eyes in an effort to drive them from its mind but knowing they're still there. It is severely malnourished, "so thin there are no calves to its legs; its belly protrudes; it lives on a half-bowl of corn meal and grease a day. It is naked. Its buttocks and thighs are a mass of festered sores, as it sits in its own excrement continually." It is also feeble-minded, perhaps because of long malnutrition and neglect. When someone comes by the room, which happens only rarely, the child – who hasn't spent its whole life in the room but "can remember sunlight and its mother's voice" – says, "Please let me out. I will be good!" Long ago, when it was first locked in the room, the child would cry and scream, but now it merely emits an occasional whine: "eh-haa, eh-haa."

The wretchedness of this child is heartrending. Perhaps even more heartrending, though, is that everyone in Omelas knows about the child – and does nothing to help it. How could a flourishing and happy city like Omelas permit one of its own to suffer in such horrific conditions? It's not that the people of Omelas lack empathy. On the contrary, they have as much empathy as anyone. When they learn about the child – which usually happens when they're around ten years old, the same age as the child – they're "shocked and sickened" and "would like to do something for the child." But they also understand that "there is nothing they can do." For they know that "their happiness, the beauty of their city, the tenderness of their friendships, the health of their children, the wisdom of their scholars, the skill of their makers, even the abundance of their harvest and the kindly weathers of their skies, depend wholly on this child's abominable misery." If they were to help the child in any way – by releasing it from the basement, or even by speaking a kind word to it – all of the happiness Omelas enjoys "would wither and be destroyed." The people of Omelas all know this – and so they don't help the child. But it's not out of selfishness that they don't help. Any one of the people of Omelas might gladly sacrifice her own happiness to help the child. The problem is that at stake isn't just the happiness of that one individual. At stake is the happiness of thousands. Besides, little could be done to help the child in any case. Even if it were set free, "it would not get much good of its freedom: a little vague pleasure of warmth and food, no doubt, but little more. It is too degraded and imbecile to know any real joy. It has been afraid too long ever to be free of fear." Feeling "anger, outrage, impotence," some people leave the city, never to come back – these are "the ones who walk away from Omelas." But this is the most anyone does. The child remains in the basement. Its suffering continues.

The people of Omelas abide by an ethical theory called utilitarianism. According to this theory, the morally best actions are those that maximize overall happiness. To maximize overall happiness, however, isn't necessarily to make everyone happy, for making everyone happy often isn't possible. Instead, it's to bring as much happiness into the world as possible. Suppose, for instance, that 100,000 people live in Omelas. Of these 100,000 people, one – the child in the basement – is supremely unhappy, while the remaining 99,999 are supremely happy. When we subtract the unhappiness of the one from the happiness of the many, we end up with a lot of net happiness. From a utilitarian perspective, that's good. If, on the other hand, the people of Omelas were to release the child from the basement, the child's happiness would increase but everyone else's would disappear. The result would be a net decrease in happiness. From a utilitarian perspective, this would be bad. Consequently, utilitarianism seems to imply that keeping the child locked in the basement is the right thing to do.

Utilitarianism also asserts that happiness is the only thing that has value in itself. Other things may have value, but, if they do, they have value only insofar as they increase happiness. If, for instance, religion or *drooz* increases happiness, then and only then would each have value. Similarly, respect for human rights may have value – but only if it increases happiness. Utilitarians might agree that respecting human rights usually increases happiness, but "The Ones Who Walk Away from Omelas" seems to show, in dramatic form, that exceptions occur. For releasing the child from the basement, which would respect the child's right to liberty, doesn't increase, but decreases, the overall happiness.

The point of Le Guin's story, then, is to offer a critique of utilitarianism. On the one hand, utilitarians, it seems, would have to agree that keeping the child in the basement is the right thing to do, even though this violates the child's rights. On the other hand, though, Le Guin's intuition, an intuition she expects her readers to share, is that keeping the child in the basement is morally wrong. Making people happy, we think, is good, but respecting human rights is even more important. If we must choose between the two, we must come down on the side of respecting human rights. Utilitarianism, therefore, seems to support what is morally wrong. Any ethical theory that supports what is morally wrong must be a flawed theory. Consequently, utilitarianism must be a flawed theory.

Questions for reflection: In what respects does the fictional city of Omelas resemble the real world? If we were living in Omelas and we knew of the suffering of the child in the basement, what, if anything, should we do? Is it ever justified to violate someone's rights for the sake of a greater good? Is utilitarianism a flawed ethical theory, or does it accurately capture what is morally right and what is morally wrong?

Puzzle 3
Noble Lie

Still shaking their heads in disbelief, Immanuel and Isaac shut the door behind them. They were now in Immanuel's home, after taking the ten-minute walk from the theater, where they'd been watching a ballet. The ballet was a disaster. The musicians were out of sync, and the plot was dull. One of the dancers nearly fell while pirouetting, and his costume, vulgarly garish like all the others, was visibly stained. During the swordfight scene, just as the hero was about to drive his sword through the villain, the blade came loose and clattered comically to the floor. Immanuel and Isaac couldn't sit through to the end. They left during the intermission.

Immanuel and Isaac were good friends, despite their different religious backgrounds. Whereas Isaac was Jewish, Immanuel was a pious Christian. Immanuel, though, was unlike the Nazis who had recently come into power. He believed that all persons, whatever religion they practiced, had intrinsic value and, as such, should be treated with respect. Persons were different from things. Things – such as a hammer or pencil – had only instrumental value. They could be used as mere means to achieve whatever ends one liked. A hammer could be used as a means to build a house; a pencil could be used as a means to write a grocery list. Neither the hammer nor the pencil had any say in the matter. Persons, though, should never be used as mere means. They shouldn't, for example, be raped, or stolen from, or murdered. Persons had moral rights; things didn't. Immanuel could never discriminate against Jews, the way the Nazis did.

As Isaac was settling down on Immanuel's living room sofa and Immanuel was hanging up their coats, Immanuel heard an insistent knock at the door. It was his neighbor Hermann, a member of the Nazi Party and a known troublemaker. When Immanuel opened the door, he saw that Hermann had worked himself into a passionate fury. "I hear you know a Jew by the name of Isaac," Hermann said to Immanuel, brandishing a pistol. "Where is he? I'm going to shoot him like a dog!"

Immanuel was taken aback, but had no reason to doubt Hermann's sincerity. Even the mildest of the Nazis disliked Jewish people, and Hermann wasn't the mildest of the Nazis. Immanuel had seen Hermann threaten Jews, spit on them, and call them vile names. He had even heard that Hermann had murdered a Jewish family – with impunity. Now that the Nazis were in power, such things could happen.

Immanuel had to think quickly. What should he do? What should he say? One possibility was to reason with Hermann, to tell him that killing Isaac would be a violation of Isaac's right to life, as well as a violation of one of the Ten Commandments: "Thou shalt not kill." But Immanuel could see right away that reasoning with Hermann would be futile. Hermann was in too great a fury, his hatred of Jews beyond all reason.

Another possibility was to attempt to overpower Hermann. But this, too, would be futile. Immanuel was a tiny man, no match for the hulking Hermann. Besides, Hermann was the one carrying a gun. Immanuel was unarmed.

The obvious thing to do was to tell a bald-faced lie: "I'm sorry, Hermann. I have no idea where Isaac is. Good luck finding him!" Or perhaps, "When the Nazis came into power, Isaac and his family fled to America. If you want to shoot him, you'll have to cross the Atlantic." Or some other such thing. Lying seemed to be the best way to save Isaac's life. Granted, under normal circumstances, lying wasn't a nice thing to do. But these circumstances weren't normal. Surely, letting a friend die was worse than telling a lie. Besides, did a scoundrel like Hermann have a right to the truth in any case? Plato called a lie told in a situation like this – not for one's own selfish purposes, but for a greater good – a noble lie. Plato would have had no problem lying to Hermann.

Immanuel, however, wasn't so sure. Wasn't Hermann, as horrible as he was, a person like anyone else? And wouldn't lying to him be treating him as a mere means – a means to saving Isaac's life? If treating persons as mere means was always wrong, as Immanuel thought, wouldn't lying to Hermann be wrong – no matter how good the consequences might be? It seemed to Immanuel that if he told the truth – "Isaac's right here in my living room, down the hall and to the left" – and Hermann proceeded to murder Isaac, the fault wouldn't lie with Immanuel telling the truth but instead with Hermann pulling the trigger on his pistol.

Suppose, however, that Immanuel was mistaken about this, that he'd be partly responsible if, as a result of telling the truth, Isaac died. But would lying be any better? Suppose that Immanuel lied to Hermann, and suppose that Isaac, unaware of the lie but overhearing from the living room that Hermann wanted to kill him, slipped out the back door. If Hermann were to believe the lie, might not he leave the house, spot Isaac as he was slipping out, and catch him and kill him? And if this were to happen, wouldn't Immanuel be partly responsible for Isaac's death – because it was his lie that led Hermann to leave and then spot and kill Isaac? No, Immanuel couldn't lie. Lying was always wrong.

Yet telling the truth – saying that Isaac was in the living room – didn't seem palatable either. If only Immanuel had another option, a way of telling the truth that didn't get Isaac killed. Was there such a truth? It occurred to Immanuel that there was. He could tell Hermann a misleading truth. For example, he could say, "I saw Isaac not half an hour ago at the ballet. You might look for him there." Strictly speaking, this would be true. Immanuel really did see Isaac at the ballet less than half an hour ago, and, although Hermann certainly wouldn't find Isaac at the ballet, it was true that he might look for him there. Since this was strictly speaking the truth, Immanuel wouldn't be using Hermann as a mere means to saving Isaac's life, but he would save Isaac's life – if his misleading truth sent Hermann to the ballet on a wild goose chase.

But was a misleading truth any better than an outright lie? How were they different, really? Didn't both involve an intentional deception? How could one justify the one kind of intentional deception but not the other?

Immanuel didn't have the time to mull on difficult questions such as these. He had to respond to Hermann immediately. But that was all right. Immanuel knew what to do, and he felt comfortable doing it.

Questions for reflection: How should Immanuel respond to Hermann? Are noble lies justified, or is lying always wrong? Is telling a misleading truth always wrong? Is telling the truth always the best way to respect people's rights?

Puzzle 4
Theme and Variations

The Original Trolley Problem

Philippa sees a runaway trolley hurtling down a set of tracks. No one is on board the trolley, and so no one can apply its brakes to stop it. Some distance in front of the trolley, five people are tied to the tracks, unable to move. Philippa is close enough to them that she can see their struggles, but she isn't close enough that she can untie them – the trolley will get there before she can. If she does nothing, the trolley will kill all five of the people. Right next to Philippa is a lever. If she pulls the lever, the trolley will divert to a side track, thereby saving the five people. However, some distance down the side track is one more person, tied and unable to move. So, if Philippa pulls the lever, this other person will die. What should Philippa do? Should she pull the lever, or should she not pull the lever? Why?

Variation 1: The Heavy Stranger

Philippa sees a runaway trolley hurtling down a set of tracks. No one is on board the trolley, and so no one can apply its brakes to stop it. Some distance in front of the trolley, five people are tied to the tracks, unable to move. Philippa is close enough to them that she can see their struggles, but she isn't close enough that she can untie them – the trolley will get there before she can. If she does nothing, the trolley will kill all five of the people. Philippa stands on a bridge overlooking the tracks. There is no lever that she can pull, diverting the trolley to a side track, but standing next to her is a very heavy man wearing a very heavy backpack. The heavy man is unknown to Philippa, an innocent bystander, minding his own business, unaware of the oncoming trolley or the five people tied to the tracks. Philippa can save these five people, but only if she pushes the heavy man with his heavy backpack off the bridge and onto the tracks. Then the trolley will crash into the heavy man, killing him, but the man is heavy enough that the trolley will stop there. There is no other way that Philippa can save the five people tied to the tracks. What should Philippa do? Should she push the heavy man off the bridge? Why or why not?

Variation 2: The Heavy Villain

Philippa sees a runaway trolley hurtling down a set of tracks. No one is on board the trolley, and so no one can apply its brakes to stop it. Some distance in front of the trolley, five people are tied to the tracks, unable to move. Philippa is close enough to them that she can see their struggles, but she isn't close enough that she can untie them – the trolley will get there before she can. If she does nothing, the trolley will kill all five of the people. Philippa stands on a bridge overlooking the track. There is no lever that she can pull, diverting the trolley to another track, but standing next to her is a very heavy man wearing a very heavy backpack. The heavy man is responsible for tying the five people to the tracks – he's a horrible sadist who enjoys watching trolleys squash people. Philippa can save these five people, but only if she pushes the heavy man with his heavy backpack off the bridge and onto the tracks. Then the trolley will crash into the heavy man, killing him, but the man is heavy enough that the trolley will stop there. There is no other way that Philippa can save the five people tied to the tracks. What should Philippa do? Should she push the heavy man off the bridge? Why or why not?

Variation 3: The Heavy Son

Philippa sees a runaway trolley hurtling down a set of tracks. No one is on board the trolley, and so no one can apply its brakes to stop it. Some distance in front of the trolley, five people are tied to the tracks, unable to move. Philippa is close enough to them that she can see their struggles, but she isn't close enough that she can untie them – the trolley will get there before she can. If she does nothing, the trolley will kill all five of the people. Philippa stands on a bridge overlooking the track. There is no lever that she can pull, diverting the trolley to another track, but standing next to her is a very heavy man wearing a very heavy backpack. The heavy man is her son, whom she loves with all her heart – he's not a horrible sadist who enjoys watching trolleys squash people. Philippa can save these five people, but only if she pushes her son with his heavy backpack off the bridge and onto the tracks. Then the trolley will crash into her son, killing him, but her son is heavy enough that the trolley will stop there. There is no other way that Philippa can save the five people tied to the tracks. What should Philippa do? Should she push her son off the bridge? Why or why not?

Variation 4: The Nuclear Warhead

Philippa sees a runaway trolley hurtling down a set of tracks. No people are on board the trolley, but a nuclear warhead is. Placed there by terrorists, the nuclear warhead is set to go off just as the trolley reaches a nearby city. If Philippa does nothing, the explosion will kill several million people. Philippa stands on a bridge overlooking the tracks. There is no lever that she can pull, diverting the trolley to a side track, but standing next to her is a very heavy man wearing a very heavy backpack. The heavy man is unknown to Philippa, an innocent bystander, minding his own business, unaware of the oncoming trolley and the nuclear warhead on board. Philippa can save the city and its several million inhabitants, but only if she pushes the heavy man with his heavy backpack off the bridge and onto the tracks. Then the trolley will crash into the heavy man, killing him, but the man is heavy enough that the trolley will stop there, before it reaches the city. There is no other way that Philippa can save the city and its several million inhabitants. What should Philippa do? Should she push the heavy man off the bridge? Why or why not?

Variation 5: The Man in a Hammock

Philippa sees a runaway trolley hurtling down a set of tracks. No one is on board the trolley, and so no one can apply its brakes to stop it. Some distance in front of the trolley, five people are tied to the tracks, unable to move. Philippa is close enough to them that she can see their struggles, but she isn't close enough that she can untie them – the trolley will get there before she can. If she does nothing, the trolley will kill all five of the people. Right next to Philippa is a lever. If she pulls the lever, a second trolley, empty like the first, will crash into the first trolley, and both trolleys will derail and come crashing down a hill. The five people will be saved. However, at the bottom of the hill, a man is in his backyard, taking a nap in his hammock. He will be killed. What should Philippa do? Should she pull the lever, or should she not pull the lever? Why?

Variation 6: The Quintuple Transplant

Philippa is an organ transplant surgeon. In her hospital are five patients, each needing a different organ. Without a transplant, the five patients will die. A stranger visits the town, coming via trolley, and stops by the hospital for a checkup. Upon examining the stranger, Philippa notices that his organs are a perfect match for her five patients. Philippa knows how to arrange things so that, if the stranger were to disappear, no one would suspect that she was involved. She also knows that there is no other way she can save her five patients. What should Philippa do, and why?

Variation 7: The Bugatti

Nearing retirement, Philippa invests the bulk of her life savings in a rare old car, a Bugatti. Although the Bugatti has a very high value, she has not yet been able to have the car insured. Philippa loves her Bugatti. Not only is it a joy for her to drive and take care of the car, but she knows that its market value is rising, so that, if the need arises, she can sell it and live in comfort after she retires. One day Philippa parks her Bugatti by the end of a railway siding and takes a stroll up the trolley track. As she walks, she sees a runaway trolley, with no one aboard, hurtling down the track. Farther down the track, she sees a child playing, whom the runaway trolley will likely kill. She has no way to stop the trolley and the child is too far away to hear her shouts of warning, but beside her is a lever that, if she pulls, will divert the trolley down the siding where she parked her Bugatti. Pulling the lever will save the child – but the trolley will crash into her Bugatti, destroying it. Thinking of the pleasure the car gives her and the financial security it promises, Philippa chooses not to throw the switch. The child dies. For many more years, Philippa enjoys her Bugatti. Did Philippa do the right thing? Why or why not?

Questions for reflection: How would a utilitarian, seeking to maximize overall happiness, solve the different versions of the trolley problem? How would a Kantian, treating persons always as ends and never as mere means, solve the different versions of the trolley problem? Do either of these approaches to the trolley problem provide good solutions?

Puzzle 5
Price Gouging

In August 2004, Floridians were walloped with a one-two punch. The first punch was delivered by Charley, a category 4 hurricane, which, after churning in the Gulf of Mexico, slammed into the Florida peninsula, killing fifteen people and causing $16.9 billion in damage. The second punch, coming in the days and weeks following Charley's departure into the Atlantic, was an epidemic of price gouging.

The cost of many basic necessities – from bottled water and gasoline to generators and tar paper for roof repair – spiked sharply. Ice, which had previously sold for two dollars a bag, was now going for ten dollars a bag. The price of gasoline jumped from $1.78 to three dollars a gallon. Small generators for homes quadrupled in price, from $250 to $1,000. A contractor offered to clear two trees from the roof of a woman's house – for $23,000. A man who sought refuge for himself and his family at the Days Inn Airport Hotel in West Palm Beach found two available rooms and a sign that said all rooms were $39.99 – yet he was charged $109. Some Floridians, such as the woman who needed two trees cleared from her roof, refused to pay the outrageous prices, but others, such as the man who showed up at the Days Inn Airport Hotel, felt they had no choice.

Many Floridians were incensed. Charlie Crist, the state's attorney general, who would later become governor of Florida, summed up the anger: "It is astounding to me, the level of greed that someone must have in their soul to be willing to take advantage of someone suffering in the wake of a hurricane." To this sentiment, Crist added, "This is not the normal free market situation where willing buyers freely elect to enter into the marketplace and meet willing sellers, where a price is agreed upon based on supply and demand. In an emergency, buyers under duress have no freedom. Their purchases of necessities like safe lodging are forced." Thousands of claims were filed with the attorney general's office, some of which were successfully prosecuted under Florida's law against price gouging. The Days Inn Airport Hotel, for example, had to pay restitution plus $70,000 in penalties.

The case for laws against price gouging is powerful, for such laws appear to promote three important values: welfare, freedom, and virtue.

Welfare. As Crist pointed out, Floridians were already "suffering in the wake of a hurricane." Charging exorbitant prices must only have exacerbated this suffering. Suppose a hurricane has rendered your home unsafe – perhaps the drenching rain has flooded it, or fallen trees have damaged it. The repairs will cost thousands of dollars, even with fair prices, and may drain your life savings. Then you flee to a hotel that charges you $109 for a room that just a few days before cost only $39.99. The high price isn't going to enhance your welfare, or help you get your life back in order. But because of Florida's law against price gouging, which requires vendors to sell at reasonable prices, you're able to recover your loss. In this way, Florida's law appears to promote welfare.

Freedom. As Crist also pointed out, "buyers under duress have no freedom." For example, Floridians who, because of the hurricane, lost access to clean drinking water had little choice but to purchase bottled water, no matter its price. Similarly, families who lost power, and hence air conditioning, in their homes may have been forced to fork over $1,000 for a generator to get them through the sweltering August heat. Price gouging thus more closely resembles extortion than the free exchange of goods and services. Insofar as it discourages price gouging, Florida's law appears to promote freedom.

Virtue. Crist lamented "the level of greed that [price gougers] must have in their soul." Instead of profiting at the expense of those of our neighbors who endure hardship, we should lend them a helping hand. Helping others in need is a virtue that any society should promote; greed is a vice that any society should discourage. But Florida's law against price gouging is aimed at discouraging greed. It therefore appears to discourage vice and promote virtue.

Not everyone, however, agreed with Crist. According to economist Thomas Sowell, for instance, price gouging is an "emotionally powerful but economically meaningless" term, one that "most economists pay no attention to, because it seems too confused to begin with." Jeff Jacoby, a pro-market contributor to the *Boston Globe*, concurred, claiming that price gouging is merely a "pejorative and destructive name" for the laws of supply and demand, and that the laws of supply and demand, far from an evil that should be eradicated through legislation, are simply "the way the world works." "Why should it be news, let alone a crime," Jacoby asked, "when soaring demand and/or tight supplies send prices through the roof?" In defense of their position, Sowell and Jacoby responded to Crist's appeal to welfare, freedom, and virtue.

Welfare. Imagine that Florida adopts a free-market economy, one in which prices are determined solely by the laws of supply and demand. In this imaginary Florida, the government doesn't pass or enforce any laws against price gouging, nor does it do anything else to control prices. A hurricane strikes, with the result that the demand for generators increases sharply. Initially, the supply isn't equal to the demand, so the cost of a generator goes up – perhaps it quadruples from $250 to $1,000. But according to Sowell and Jacoby, the price increase is only temporary. Manufacturers of generators in states not affected by the hurricane – Georgia or Alabama, say – will notice the increased demand and will understand that they'll be able to sell more generators if they bring them into Florida. They may not be especially concerned about the welfare of the Floridians who need generators. They just want to make some money. But by taking their business into Florida, the supply of generators in Florida increases, and the price of generators consequently decreases. Floridians get the generators they need at a reasonable price, which enhances their welfare.

Contrast this free-market Florida with a Florida that effectively enforces a law against price gouging. A hurricane strikes; the demand for generators spikes. In fear of the law against price gouging, the local manufacturers of generators continue to sell generators for $250. But they don't have enough generators to meet the increased demand. Nor will manufacturers of generators from Georgia or Alabama have motivation to bring their generators into Florida. Doing so won't be profitable, because the $250 they'll get for each generator they sell won't be worth the cost of transporting the generators such a distance. The result of this is that many Floridians have to forgo the generators they need, and this doesn't enhance their welfare. As Jacoby put it, "Demonizing vendors won't speed Florida's recovery. Letting them go about their business will."

Freedom. Sowell and Jacoby, as well as other advocates of a free-market economy, highly prize freedom. In their view, all people should be free to do anything they want, except interfere with other people's similar freedom. This includes business owners, who should be free to run their businesses as they see fit, without interference from the government. But laws against price gouging are government interference with the freedom of business owners, forcing business owners to set lower prices when they may wish to set higher prices. Laws against price gouging therefore violate business owners' right to liberty, and for this reason they should be done away with.

But what about the man who was forced to pay $109 for a room at the Days Inn Airport Hotel? Didn't the owner of the hotel interfere with his freedom, violating his right to liberty? Not at all, according to advocates of a free-market economy. On the contrary, by charging $109 rather than $39.99, the owner of the hotel may have increased this man's freedom. Notice that, when the man arrived at the hotel, only two rooms were available. If the owner of the hotel had been charging the usual $39.99, those two rooms may have been more attractive to Floridians seeking shelter and may have been snatched up long before the man arrived. If this had happened, he wouldn't have had the freedom to obtain a room at the hotel – and, if other hotels similarly charged their usual prices, he may not have been able to obtain a room at any hotel. Instead of complaining about price gouging, perhaps he should have been grateful that he was able to get anything at all.

Virtue. According to defenders of a free-market economy, the freedom business owners enjoy should include the freedom to choose the virtues they'd like their businesses to embody. Some business owners, for example, might wish to adopt the virtue of charity. In times of emergency, such as when a hurricane strikes, these business owners might wish to give away the generators they manufacture, or sell them at a modest price. But other business owners might believe that charity is a vice rather than a virtue, arguing that it only encourages laziness among its recipients – why, after all, should people work hard if they can get by on charity? These business owners might prefer to sell their generators at the highest price the market will bear. Both sorts of business owners may mean well, and both may have important arguments in support of their preferences. In a pluralist society such as the United States, respect for such diversity of values is imperative, and the way to respect it is to allow business owners to express their values in their businesses. The government, which has no special insight into what counts as a virtue and what counts as a vice, shouldn't, in the form of laws against price gouging, force business owners to adopt what *it* values.

Questions for reflection: Should there be laws against price gouging? Do laws against price gouging promote — or do they interfere with — welfare, freedom, and virtue? Do they respect human rights, or violate them?

Puzzle 6
The State of Nature

Thomas: A State of War

Thomas peers through some bushes at a grassy clearing. Several people are already there, terrified, warily circling each other, their fists, white-knuckled, clutching makeshift weapons – a jagged rock, a sturdy branch, the femur of a good-sized animal. They, like Thomas, are a sorry-looking lot, grimy and disheveled, their cheeks sunken and ribs protruding, some naked, others clad in crude costumes made of leaves or animal skins. All of them are homeless, and all of them are young. There are no old people in the state of nature.

The state of nature is a state of anarchy – a condition of life that features no government, no laws, and no police to enforce laws. If Thomas robs, rapes, or murders, he won't be arrested, put on trial, and punished. He won't be jailed, fined, or forced to undergo community service. In the state of nature, he's free to do to others whatever he likes, and others are free to do to him whatever they like.

A short while ago, for instance, as he wandered through the forest foraging for food, Thomas spied a girl, perhaps ten years old, plucking an apple from an apple tree. The apple, the first to appear on the tree that season, was small and green, not yet ripe, but when one is hungry, as the girl was, one takes what one can get. However, as she was about to bite into the apple, a man, approaching from her rear, flung himself at her in a fury. In the scuffle that followed, the apple fell to the ground. Taking advantage of the opportunity, Thomas swept in, snatched the apple, bit off half of it, and – the sourness making his face pucker – quickly swallowed. By then, the man who had attacked the girl started running after Thomas. Because he was larger and faster than Thomas, Thomas opted for the prudent course of action, dropping the half-eaten apple and running for cover. Out of the corner of his eye, he saw the man pounce on the prized fruit. Behind the man, the girl lay unmoving. She may have been merely stunned, or she may have been dead.

Thomas doesn't feel sorry for the girl, and it would never have occurred to him to come to her aid. Only one thing about the incident troubles him – he wishes he could have eaten the whole apple. The only interests he seeks to satisfy are his own; the interests of others, unless they help him satisfy his own interests, are irrelevant. But didn't the girl have a right to the apple, since she was the one who plucked it from the tree? No. In the state of nature, no one has a right to anything. In the state of nature, right and wrong have no existence, but come into existence only with the establishment of a civil society and the passage of laws. Stealing, for example, is wrong only when there is a law against stealing. Before the law is passed, as in the state of nature, stealing isn't wrong.

Thomas peers again through the bushes. A larger crowd has now gathered in the clearing, shuffling about, their weapons to the ready in case of trouble. Thomas, too, carries weapons, a stick in one hand and a rock in the other. Although he likes his freedom – the freedom to do anything whatever – he can't trust anyone. An attack can come at any time and in any place. The state of nature is dangerous, a war of everyone against everyone else. In such a condition, there is no place for industry, because the fruit thereof is uncertain. Consequently, there is no culture of the earth, no navigation or use of the commodities that may be imported by sea, no commodious building, no instruments of moving and removing such things as require much force, no knowledge of the face of the earth, no account of time, no arts, no letters, no society – and worst of all, continual fear and danger of violent death, and the life of human beings, solitary, poor, nasty, brutish, and short.

It's ironic, Thomas thinks to himself, that we in the state of nature seek to satisfy only our own interests, but in so doing utterly fail to satisfy our own interests. But all is not hopeless. Human beings possess a special faculty that no other species has – the faculty of reason. Reason will find a solution to the problem. Indeed, that's what the meeting in the grassy clearing is all about. The people there will make an agreement – call it the social contract – in which they will give up the freedom they enjoy in the state of nature, but in return will gain security. The way to achieve security is to form a government that has the power to pass and enforce laws. People will think twice before robbing, raping, or murdering because they know that, if they get caught, they'll pay a heavy price. The government will need to be powerful too, the more powerful the better – a monarch with absolute power will be best. True, a powerful monarch might exploit the people over whom he or she rules, but this is better than the alternative, a weak government that is easily overthrown, in which case the commonwealth would revert to the state of nature. Nothing, Thomas concludes, is worse than the state of nature.

Thomas steps out from behind the bushes and joins the others in the grassy clearing. Like them, he's wary, but he's also optimistic. He's ready to agree to the social contract. He's ready to leave the state of nature.

John: A State of Insecurity

John peers through the window of his house at a grassy field. Several people are already there, milling about, uneasy but not terrified. A few of them greet each other with a nod of the head or a clasp of the hands; a few of them carry a knife, pistol, or other weapon. Like John, they're neither rich nor poor, most of them living in modest houses, most of them adequately clothed, wearing simple shoes and simple tunics, and most of them adequately fed. Some are young, others old. There are old people in the state of nature.

The state of nature is a state of anarchy – a condition of life that features no government, no laws, and no police to enforce laws. If John robs, rapes, or murders, he won't be arrested, put on trial, and punished. He won't be jailed, fined, or forced to undergo community service. Yet, though the state of nature is a state of freedom, it's not a state of license to do anything whatever.

A short while ago, for instance, as he was strolling through the neighborhood, John spied a girl, perhaps ten years old, plucking an apple from an apple tree. The apple, large and heavy and red, appeared sweet and juicy. John would have liked to eat that apple. Although he could have picked any of the other apples that hung from the tree, those apples didn't seem as ripe or delicious as the apple the girl held in her hand. He was tempted to snatch it from her. He was pretty sure he could pull it off, as she was all by herself and he was much larger and stronger than she was. But he didn't give in to the temptation. He knew the apple belonged to her – it became her property the moment she plucked it from the tree, mixing her labor with it. As he passed by the girl, she took a bite of her apple, the juice dribbling down her chin and her face beaming pleasure.

John has no regrets about the incident. While the girl had no *legal* right to the apple, since in the state of nature no government exists to bestow legal rights, she nonetheless had a *moral* right to it. Even in the state of nature, people have moral rights – to life, liberty, and property

– and these moral rights must be respected. Stealing, for example, isn't wrong only when the government passes a law against stealing. Stealing is wrong even before such a law is passed. The state of nature has a moral, if not a government-created, law to govern it, which obliges everyone. This moral law states that, because all are equal in the state of nature, no one having authority over another, people are morally required not to harm others in their lives, liberties, or properties.

John peers again through the window of his house. A larger crowd has now gathered in the field, shuffling about, their weapons to the ready in case of trouble. John, too, carries a weapon, a pistol that he keeps tucked in the folds of his tunic. Although he likes his freedom – the freedom to do anything within the bounds of the moral law – he can't trust people. All too often, instead of obeying the moral law, people obey their appetites, harming others in their lives, liberties, or properties because they perceive that doing so will advance their own interests. To be sure, the state of nature isn't so awful that it's a state of war of everyone against everyone else, but it's not good either, because it's a state of insecurity. Some people fare tolerably well into their old age; others don't.

John would like something better than the state of nature offers, and he knows how to get it. Human beings possess a special faculty that no other species has – the faculty of reason. Reason will find a solution to the problem. Indeed, that's what the meeting in the grassy field is all about. The people there will make an agreement – call it the social contract – in which they will give up the freedom they enjoy in the state of nature, but in return will gain security. The way to achieve security is to form a government that has the power to pass and enforce laws. People will think twice before robbing, raping, or murdering because they know that, if they get caught, they'll pay a heavy price. The government shouldn't be too powerful, though – a monarch with limited power will be best. True, a less powerful government is more easily overthrown, in which case the commonwealth would revert to the state of nature. But that's all right. The state of nature, with its insecurity, is better than a powerful monarch who exploits the people over whom he or she rules. Besides, government has no legitimate power beyond what the social contract authorizes, and the social contract authorizes government only to protect people's rights to life, liberty, and property. If government does anything beyond this, it violates the social contract, and, the contract becoming void, the people have a right to overthrow their government and institute a new one.

John steps out of his house and joins the others in the grassy field. Like them, he's wary, but he's also optimistic. He's ready to agree to the social contract. He's ready to leave the state of nature.

Questions for reflection: What would life be like without any government, laws, or police to enforce laws? Would life in the state of nature be a state of war of everyone against everyone else? Would it instead be merely a state of insecurity? Should there be a government? What is the proper role of government? Under what circumstances, if any, do people have a right to overthrow their government?

Puzzle 7
Veil of Ignorance

J. R. wasn't sure what to expect. She'd been selected to participate in a philosophical experiment, but she had little idea what a philosophical experiment was. Once, when she was an undergraduate student, she had signed up for a philosophy course – she thought it would be interesting because it was about human rights, something she strongly believed in. She dropped the course after a week, however, because she found the material dismayingly abstract – and because the instructor took sadistic delight in giving students endless pop quizzes. Now, thirty years later, J. R. had still never known the pleasure of taking part in a philosophical experiment.

The room she entered was an ordinary classroom – not a laboratory, as she had half expected. Dozens of people, presumably other participants in the experiment, were already there, some of them seated, others milling about and conversing with each other. They were a diverse group, men and women of different ages, different racial and ethnic backgrounds, and – if J. R. could judge by the clothes and accessories they wore – different socioeconomic status. J. R. took a seat near the front, so that she could hear better – several years ago, in an accident, she had sustained some loss of hearing in her left ear. As she sat, she noticed the cup of water and array of pills – each a different shape and color – that were placed on her desk. When she glanced around, she saw that the other desks were similarly equipped.

She wondered for a moment what the pills might be for, until a man wearing oversized, dark-rimmed glasses entered the room and stood at the podium up front. He gave people a moment to take their seats, and then he introduced himself. He was a philosopher at Harvard University, and he'd be conducting the experiment. He explained that the experiment would be about distributive justice. Contrasting with retributive justice – which dealt with issues relating to punishment and war, such as whether the death penalty should be abolished or whether dropping the bomb on Hiroshima was justified – distributive justice was the area of justice concerned with how the benefits and burdens of society should be distributed. The benefits of society were whatever people got from society – for example, their salary, education, and health care. In contrast, the burdens of society were whatever people gave to society, such as the taxes they paid and the work they did for a living. The goal of today's experiment was to figure out how these benefits and burdens should be distributed – who should get what, and who should give what. Was it fair that some people were billionaires while others were homeless? Would it be better if everyone received the same income, no matter how much or how little they worked? Should students be able to go to college, and should the sick be able to see a doctor, for free? Should people be required to pay taxes, and, if so, how much should the wealthy pay and how much should the poor pay? The people who'd figure out answers to these and similar questions were the participants sitting in this room. They'd do this by taking a vote – a vote on what the most just distribution of benefits and burdens would be. The outcome of the vote needed to be unanimous.

J. R. was intrigued, because the questions the Harvard philosopher raised were of the highest importance. She herself felt she paid far too much in taxes and received far too little in salary. But she was also skeptical. Unanimous? How could the Harvard philosopher expect such a diverse group to reach unanimity? Wouldn't the wealthy, for example, tend to vote for a distribution favoring the wealthy – giving themselves the highest salaries, the lowest taxes, the best access to education and health care, and so on – and wouldn't the poor tend to vote for a distribution favoring the poor? Furthermore, even if – somehow – the people in this room reached unanimity, what expertise did they have on distributive justice? Why should their votes count for anything? J. R. had never given much thought to distributive justice – indeed, before today she'd never even heard the expression "distributive justice." She didn't think she'd be up to the task that the Harvard philosopher was setting, and she suspected that the other participants were in no better a position than she.

The philosopher seemed to anticipate J. R.'s skepticism. To be able, he said, to figure out what the most just distribution of benefits and burdens would be, the participants would have to have a number of characteristics. Some of these characteristics they probably already had, at least to some degree. Others they certainly didn't have. Not to worry, though. Before the vote took place, he'd help the participants acquire all the characteristics they needed. He then listed the necessary characteristics.

First, the participants would need to have a sense of justice – an ability to judge some things just and other things unjust, and an ability to support these judgments with reasons. Without such abilities, the participants wouldn't be able to recognize, much less vote for, the most just distribution of benefits and burdens. The good news was that nearly all human beings, once they reached a certain age, had a sense of justice. But the philosopher didn't want to leave anything to chance, so he asked that all participants swallow the round white pill that was sitting on their desks. This pill – a marvel of science developed specifically for this experiment – would give everyone a sense of justice. The pill, the philosopher added, was absolutely safe, and its effect would be temporary, lasting only long enough for the participants to vote. Still skeptical, J. R. placed the little white pill on the back of her tongue, took a drink from her cup of water, and swallowed. The pill didn't make her feel any different, but perhaps that was because she already had a sense of justice.

Second, the participants would need to be rational. To figure out what the most just distribution would be, they'd need to be able to assess the arguments for and against the various contending distributions – and such an assessment would require rationality. Just as nearly all of the participants already had a sense of justice, so nearly all had some degree of rationality. But no doubt some were less rational than others, and so the philosopher asked everyone to take the hexagonal yellow pill, which was designed to boost rationality. Dutifully, J. R. swallowed the pill. A few minutes later, she felt remarkably clear-headed. She liked the sensation.

Third, the participants would need to have complete knowledge of the facts of human psychology. They'd need to know, for example, that most human beings would rather have a larger than a smaller share of goods. Such knowledge was important because it would allow the participants to determine which distributions were compatible with human nature. If a distribution were incompatible with human nature – psychologically impossible for human beings to implement – there wouldn't be any point voting for it, no matter how just the distribution may seem. In accordance with the philosopher's instructions, J. R. took the square red pill. Within minutes, she knew everything about human psychology. She liked this sensation as well, and hoped – despite what the philosopher had said – that its effect would be permanent.

Fourth, the participants would need to be under a veil of ignorance – that is, although they now knew all the general facts of human psychology, they wouldn't be permitted to know anything specific about themselves. They couldn't, for instance, know whether they were Democrats or Republicans, Christians or Muslims, employed or unemployed, brown-eyed or blue-eyed. People who knew they had brown eyes might be tempted to vote for a distribution favoring brown-eyed people, while people who knew they had blue eyes might be tempted to vote for a distribution favoring blue-eyed people. Such votes, however, would be arbitrary, grounded not in justice, as the philosopher was aiming for, but in naked self-interest. Hence the cylindrical blue pill, a sort of amnesia pill, which would place the participants under the veil of ignorance.

J. R. hesitated. She wasn't eager to lose all the knowledge she had of herself, but when the philosopher reminded the participants that the amnesia would only be temporary and that the experiment was for a good cause, J. R. swallowed the pill. Soon she forgot everything she knew about herself. She couldn't remember that she was an African American, a woman, a mother of three daughters, a divorcee, a fifty-year-old, an atheist, and a hair stylist. She also forgot that she was hard of hearing in her left ear and that she had once signed up for a philosophy course only to drop it a week after the semester had begun. She even forgot that she'd taken any pills. After all, if she knew that she'd taken an amnesia pill, she might be tempted to vote for a distribution giving takers of amnesia pills a high salary and top-of-the-line health care.

J. R. didn't know whether she took any pills after the amnesia pill – if she took some, she immediately forgot. But she did know one thing. After swallowing all the pills the philosopher had asked her to swallow, she knew precisely how to arrive at the most just distribution of the benefits and burdens of society. It was simple, really, like child's play. Obviously, a society should adopt two principles of distributive justice. The first principle was about how much freedom people should have: Each person should be free to pursue whatever plan of life he or she wanted, as long as others had a similar freedom to pursue their plans of life. J. R. no longer knew what her plan of life was – the amnesia pill assured that – but she figured that, no matter what it was, she'd like a maximum of freedom to pursue it. She wanted, for example, to be free to listen to the music of Metallica, or to dance the cancan in a bikini, because, for all she knew, she might have an interest in those things. But of course, it cut both ways: if she was to be free to pursue her plan of life, she must let others be free to pursue their plans of life. Thus, she shouldn't be free to kill or rob others, because that would limit their freedom.

The second principle permitted an unequal distribution of benefits and burdens, but only if two conditions were met. First, positions and offices must be open to all. To deny high-paying positions to racial or religious minorities, for example, or to deny women the right to run for political office, would clearly be an injustice. Equal opportunity was essential. Second, an unequal distribution must be to the advantage of the least well off members of society. For illustration, J. R. imagined three possible distributions of the annual salaries of three employees at an accounting firm – a partner, a staff accountant, and a cleaning person:

	Distribution 1	Distribution 2	Distribution 3
Partner	$50,000	$250,000	$90,000
Staff Accountant	$50,000	$35,000	$75,000
Cleaning Person	$50,000	$15,000	$60,000

Since J. R. was under the veil of ignorance, she didn't know whether she worked at an accounting firm, and, if she did, she didn't know whether she was the partner, the staff accountant, or the cleaning person. But she knew that, if she had any say in what the annual salaries of these three people would be, she'd choose Distribution 3 over Distributions 1 and 2. Distribution 2 was a gamble. If she turned out to be the partner she'd win big, but if she happened to be the cleaning person she'd have to struggle to make ends meet. She didn't want to take that kind of risk. Distribution 1 was less of a gamble, and hence better, than Distribution 2, but it wasn't as good as Distribution 3, because everyone, including the least well off cleaning person, was better off in Distribution 3 than in Distribution 1. The second principle of distributive justice also favored Distribution 3. According to the second principle, the most just distribution would be the equal one – that is, Distribution 1 – unless an unequal distribution was to the advantage of the least well off person. Since the least well off person – namely, the cleaning person – was better off in Distribution 3 than in Distributions 1 and 2, Distribution 3 must be the most just distribution.

J. R. was ready for the vote. So were all the other participants. When all the ballots were counted, the vote turned out to be unanimous, just as the philosopher had predicted.

Questions for reflection: How should the benefits and burdens of society be distributed? Should they be distributed equally? Is anything wrong with a world in which some people are billionaires while others go hungry? Should society help its least well off members become better off?

Puzzle 8
Abduction, Rape, and Forced Marriage

Aberew Jemma had never spoken to her, and she was unaware of his existence. Still, he wanted to marry her. Her name was Woinshet Zebene, and she was thirteen years old.

Fearing that her family would reject him, he acted in accordance with the custom of his culture – he gathered together four of his friends and, with their help, broke into Woinshet's hut during the middle of the night, abducted her, and casually raped and beat her over the course of two days. His behavior had a rationale. Once she was raped and lost her virginity, her community, he knew, would consider her ruined and nobody else would likely want to marry her. This increased the probability that she would agree to marry him, and that her parents would allow the marriage. They almost certainly wouldn't prosecute him, he also knew, because doing so would be a breach of tradition and their daughter's reputation would suffer. The abduction and rape of Woinshet took place in 2001 in rural Ethiopia. At the time, rape in Ethiopia couldn't be prosecuted if the rapist later married his victim. Sixty-nine percent of marriages in Ethiopia began with abduction and rape.

But Woinshet didn't want to marry her rapist, and her father, who worked in Ethiopia's capital, Addis Ababa, where there was talk of equal rights for women, supported her decision. Baffled by this attitude, and hoping to avoid a blood feud, the village elders urged Woinshet's father to allow the marriage in exchange for a couple of cows. Woinshet's father refused. He insisted that the police investigate. Only reluctantly did they comply. Realizing that, despite tradition, he might be prosecuted, Aberew once again abducted and raped Woinshet. He even took her to the local court, hoping to bully her into marrying him. When she told a court official that she had been abducted and didn't want to marry Aberew, the official expressed astonishment: "Even if you go home," he said, "Aberew will go after you again. So there's no point in resisting." Eventually, Aberew and his four accomplices were arrested and brought to trial. The judge sentenced Aberew to ten years in prison with no chance of parole and his four accomplices to eight years in prison with no chance of parole. Soon after, however, an appeals court released the five men, claiming without explanation that the "evidence suggests that the act was consensual." Most people living in Woinshet's village were angry – not with Aberew or the judge who released him, but with Woinshet, on the grounds that her disregard for their traditions was intolerable. To escape their anger, Woinshet moved to Addis Ababa with her father.

What are we to make of the Ethiopian custom of abduction, rape, and forced marriage? Do we find it appalling? Do we want to cry out, "What is wrong with these people?" Do we believe that no society should condone such a violation of human rights? If that's what we believe, then we're moral objectivists. According to moral objectivism, the truth or falsity of moral statements – such as "Abduction, rape, and forced marriage are morally wrong" – is objective, every bit as objective as, say, "The Earth revolves around the sun." The truth of "The Earth revolves around the sun" doesn't depend on which society one happens to live in. If my society denies this statement, claiming instead that the sun revolves around the Earth, you wouldn't say, "Ah, well! Your society has a valid point. For your society the sun really does revolve around the Earth, while for mine the Earth really does revolve around the sun." Instead, you might say, "I'm sorry, but your society has gotten the facts wrong, and there's ample evidence of this." If you're a moral objectivist, you'd say much the same about moral statements. The truth of "Abduction, rape, and forced marriage are morally wrong" doesn't depend on which society one happens to live in. Aberew Jemma and other people living in Ethiopia, you'd say, don't have a valid point. They're simply mistaken, and that's that.

Moral objectivism has a great deal of support among human rights advocates, who tend to believe that all human beings, no matter what society they live in, have moral rights, that all societies should respect human rights, even if some in fact don't. Most Western philosophers, too, including utilitarians, Kantians, and libertarians, are moral objectivists. According to utilitarians, we should maximize overall happiness, and any society that claims differently is in error. According to Kantians, we should treat persons always as ends and never as mere means – and this is so no matter what culture we live in. According to libertarians, all human beings – in all societies – should be free to do anything except interfere with the comparable freedom of others.[1]

A few philosophers, and some others, however, are not moral objectivists. These thinkers advocate a theory called moral relativism, which maintains that the truth or falsity of moral statements, rather than being objective and universal, depends on the society in which the statements are made. On this theory, moral statements are similar to the statement "You should drive on the right-hand side of the road," which is true in the United States but false in England. The moral statement "Abduction, rape, and forced marriage are morally wrong" is, according to moral relativists, likewise true in some societies but false in others. It's true, for example, in the United States, which professes respect for human rights, but it's false in Ethiopia.[2]

Perhaps the most famous defense of moral relativism comes down to us from the Ancient Greek historian Herodotus. Herodotus begins by pointing out that different societies promulgate different moral beliefs: "If anyone, no matter who, were given the opportunity of choosing from amongst all the nations in the world the set of beliefs which he thought best, he would inevitably, after careful consideration of their relative merits, choose that of his own country." In support of this contention, Herodotus tells the story of Darius, the king of Persia, who approached the Greeks who happened to be in his court, asking them what it would take for them to eat their dead fathers. Horrified, the Greeks, who were more inclined to cremate their dead fathers than eat them, answered that they wouldn't do it for any amount of money. Then he turned to members of the Callatiae, a tribe from India, who ate their dead fathers, and asked them what it would take for them to burn their dead fathers. The Callatiae were just as horrified as the Greeks, assuring Darius that they wouldn't burn their dead fathers under any circumstances. Thus, the culture of the Greeks promulgated

---

[1] For more on utilitarianism, see Puzzle 2. For more on Kantian ethics, see Puzzle 3. For more on libertarianism, see Puzzle 5.

[2] More precisely, moral relativists would say it's false in the Ethiopia of 2001, when Aberew abducted and raped Woinshet. Since then, Ethiopian law has changed, so that a man can now be prosecuted for raping a girl even if she later marries him. To some degree, Ethiopian culture has shifted with this shift in law.

one moral belief – that eating one's dead father is morally wrong – while the culture of the Callatiae promulgated a different moral belief – that burning one's dead father is morally wrong. From this evidence, Herodotus concludes that "custom is king" – that is, the rightness of wrongness of an action isn't objective or universal but depends on the society in which one lives.

The premise of Herodotus' argument – that different societies promulgate different moral beliefs – isn't particularly controversial. Anyone with even the most cursory knowledge of other societies already knows this. But this premise, all by itself, doesn't establish that moral relativism is correct. After all, some societies have promulgated the belief that the sun revolves around the Earth, but it doesn't follow that, for these societies, the sun really does revolve around the Earth, for these societies could be – indeed, they are – simply mistaken. Likewise, in 2001 Ethiopia promulgated the belief that abduction, rape, and forced marriage are morally permissible, but it doesn't follow that, for Ethiopia at this time, these really were permissible. Conceivably, the Ethiopians, like societies that advocate a geocentric view of the universe, were simply mistaken. Thus, to reach the conclusion that moral relativism is correct, Herodotus needs to show that moral beliefs differ importantly from scientific beliefs such as that the Earth revolves around the sun. The difference, he might claim, is that whereas objective evidence, at least in principle, can be supplied in support of scientific beliefs, no such evidence is available to support moral beliefs. What scientific experiment, or observation, could establish, for example, that abduction, rape, and forced marriage are morally wrong? If this is what Herodotus has in mind, his argument, when stated formally, comes to this:

1. Different societies promulgate different moral beliefs.
2. <u>There is no way to establish which of these moral beliefs are objectively true.</u>
3. Therefore, the truth or falsity of moral beliefs depends on the society in which they are expressed.

This might be the argument Herodotus has in mind, but, if it is, one of its premises – the second one – is far from obviously true. Utilitarians, Kantians, and libertarians, for example, would all agree that there is a way to establish which moral beliefs are objectively true. According to utilitarians, the test for determining whether a moral belief is true is whether acting in accordance with it maximizes overall happiness. According to Kantians, the test is whether acting in accordance with it treats persons as ends and not as mere means. According to libertarians, the test is whether acting in accordance with it grants people the freedom to do as they wish except interfere with other people's comparable freedom. Of course, utilitarians, Kantians, and libertarians disagree with each other about what the right test is, but they all agree that one of these tests is objectively the right one, while the others are simply mistaken. They would also likely agree that the Ethiopian custom of abduction, rape, and forced marriage is morally wrong, as it's hard to see how this custom could maximize overall happiness, treat persons as ends and not as mere means, or grant people the freedom to do as they wish except interfere with other people's comparable freedom.

> *Questions for reflection: Are moral values relative to culture? Is respect for human rights objectively better than the Ethiopian tradition of abduction, rape, and forced marriage? Should the West pressure other countries to respect human rights? What kinds of pressure are most appropriate?*

PART II
The Rights to Life, Liberty, and Property

Puzzle 9
Lifeboat

On May 19, 1884, the *Mignonette*, a fifty-two-foot yacht, set sail from Southampton, England, on its way to Australia. On board were Thomas Dudley, the captain; Edwin Stephens, first mate; Edmund Brooks, seaman; and seventeen-year-old Richard Parker, serving as cabin boy. The sea voyage was Parker's first – he had lied about his age, claiming he was eighteen, so that he could get on board, believing the experience would make a man of him. It was not, however, meant to be. Parker's first journey at sea was also his last.

A month and a half into the journey, on July 5, bad weather struck. A wave slammed into the *Mignonette*, tearing off its lee bulwark. Within five minutes, the ship sank. The four crew members managed to scramble into the thirteen-foot lifeboat but didn't have enough time to take anything with them except some navigational instruments and two tins of turnips. They had no other food, and no fresh water. They were stranded in the middle of the South Atlantic, hundreds of miles from the nearest land.

Their plan, a longshot at best, was to steer the lifeboat into a shipping lane, where they hoped a ship would pass by, spot them, and rescue them. On the first night, they had to fend off a shark with the oars of the lifeboat. On July 7 Dudley opened the first tin of turnips, and on July 9 the crew had the good fortune to haul aboard a sea turtle, which was large enough to provide each sailor with three pounds of meat. The four men not only ate every scrap of meat they could extract from the turtle, but also sucked and gnawed on the bones and leathery skin. One day, Parker fell overboard. Dudley, the only one of the four who knew how to swim, dove into the shark-infested waters and dragged the sputtering Parker back into the lifeboat. The four men's ordeal had only just begun.

Around July 15 they ran out of food – the turnips were gone, the turtle was gone, and no more creatures from the sea had made themselves available. The four sailors attempted to catch rainwater with their oilskin capes, but with little success. By July 13 they resorted to drinking their own urine. They knew that drinking seawater wouldn't help them, but on about July 20 Parker, desperately thirsty, succumbed to the temptation. Shortly after, he fell ill.

With no food or water, and having seen no rescue ships, the other men, too, were desperate. On July 23 or 24, Dudley suggested that the four of them draw lots and that the loser sacrifice his life so that the other three could feed off his flesh. When Brooks objected to the grisly idea, Dudley abandoned it. The next day, however, Dudley, speaking to Stephens, argued that Parker, who may by then have fallen into a coma, was likely going to be the first of them to die, and that killing him now would be better than waiting for him to die, because his meat would be more nutritious and his blood better to drink. In addition, unlike him and Stephens, Parker had no wife or children depending on him, and so it made sense that Parker be the one to make the sacrifice. No action, though, was taken that day.

The next morning, twenty days into their ordeal, Dudley told the dissenting Brooks to turn away and motioned to Stephens that the time had come. While Stephens held down Parker's legs, Dudley stabbed Parker in the jugular vein with a penknife, killing him. For the next four days, all three survivors, including Brooks, fed on the deceased cabin boy. Then on the following morning, as "we was having our breakfast," as Dudley put it, the German ship *Montezuma*, passing by, sighted the lifeboat and rescued the survivors.

Upon their return to England, Dudley, Stephens, and Brooks were closely questioned about what had happened. Dudley, who believed he had done nothing wrong, responded with candor. He even showed off the penknife he had used to kill Parker, and intended to keep it as a memento. He and Stephens were charged with murder. Brooks, by contrast, was let go, because he hadn't participated in the killing of Parker, even though he, like the others, had eaten Parker's flesh.

Dudley and Stephens pleaded not guilty. As the trial progressed, public sympathy lay with the defendants. Even Parker's brother, in a display of support for the three survivors, shook each of their hands.

The defense argued necessity. Parker almost certainly would have died even if Dudley hadn't killed him, since he was too sick to have been able to hang on until the *Montezuma* arrived. And if Dudley hadn't killed Parker, the other three might well have died too, since they too were in a seriously weakened condition. Surely it was better that one of them die than that all four of them perish, and surely people have a right to save their own lives, even when the only way to do so is to take someone else's life. If two men are lost at sea, each clinging to the same plank floating in the water, but the plank will support only one of them, surely one, to preserve himself, may shove the other away from the plank, even though doing so ensures the other's death.

The court rejected this argument. First, at the time Dudley killed Parker, he had no way of knowing whether doing so was necessary to save the lives of Stephens, Brooks, and himself. For all Dudley knew, the rescue ship might have arrived four hours, rather than four days, after he plunged the penknife into Parker's jugular vein, or the rescue ship might never have arrived at all. In neither case would killing Parker have done any good. In the first case, Dudley, Stephens, and Brooks would have survived even if they hadn't killed and eaten Parker. In the second case, all of them would have perished even if they had killed and eaten Parker.

Second, even if killing Parker had been necessary to save the lives of Dudley, Stephens, and Brooks, it didn't follow that killing Parker was justified. People sometimes have a duty not to save themselves. In times of war, for example, soldiers often have a duty to give their lives. If Parker had consented to being killed and eaten, perhaps Dudley and Stephens wouldn't have been guilty of murder. Parker, however, was too ill to give consent. Killing an unwilling victim, even if it is to save oneself, is murder.

Finally, finding Dudley and Stephens not guilty would set a dangerous precedent. Sailors would acquire the power of deciding who should live and who should die, and they may not be qualified to make such decisions. Finding Dudley and Stephens not guilty could, as the court stated, provide a "legal cloak for unbridled passion and atrocious crime."

Based on this reasoning, the court found Dudley and Stephens guilty of murder. Initially, the court handed down to the two sailors the death penalty, but, given the public support for the defendants, the sentence was later reduced to six months in prison.

Postscript: After his release from prison in 1885, Thomas Dudley, who never accepted the justice of his sentence, moved to Sydney, Australia, where he became a successful boat outfitter and dealer in shipping accessories. In 1900 the bubonic plague struck Sydney. Dudley was its first victim.

Questions for reflection: Did Thomas Dudley do the right thing when he killed Richard Parker? Did he violate Parker's right to life? Should he and

Stephens have been found guilty of murder? Was a six-month prison sentence too harsh? Was it too lenient?

Puzzle 10
Terri Schiavo

February 25, 1990

In the early morning, a loud thud awakens Michael Schiavo in his St. Petersburg, Florida, apartment. Scrambling out of bed, Michael discovers his twenty-six-year-old wife, Terri, by the doorway separating the bathroom from the hallway, lying face down on the floor. She isn't moving. He tries speaking to her, but she doesn't answer. He calls 9-1-1. Within minutes, the paramedics arrive. Terri, they quickly determine, is in cardiac arrest. They are able to get her heart beating again and rush her, still unconscious, to nearby Humana Northside Hospital.

The doctors treat Terri for an apparent heart attack. A blood assay reveals that she has a potassium imbalance, which the doctors suspect triggered the heart attack. Her low level of potassium, some doctors later suggest, was the result of bulimia. As a child Terri was obese – at one point, standing at 5' 3", she weighed 200 pounds – but while she was a teenager she lost 65 pounds. After that she struggled to keep her weight under control. At the time of her collapse, she was dieting, drinking ten to fifteen glasses of iced tea a day. She weighed 120 pounds.

Despite the doctors' best efforts, Terri doesn't regain consciousness.

The days and weeks following

Terri's neurologists conduct a series of tests. Does she respond to simple commands, such as "Squeeze my hand"? No. Do her eyes track moving objects? No. Do her pupils respond to light? No. Does she show signs that she recognizes her husband or her parents? No. Terri shows no signs of cognitive functioning.

CT scans reveal that Terri's cerebral cortex is severely damaged, the damage caused by a lack of oxygen to the brain during Terri's cardiac arrest. Terri's brain stem, however, is functioning. Because her brain stem is functional, Terri is able to breathe, she is able to blink, her heart is able to beat, and her body is able to go through the regular cycles of sleeping and waking.

Eventually the doctors reach a diagnosis: Terri is in a persistent vegetative state (PVS). PVS differs from both brain death and a minimally conscious state. Brain dead patients show no brain activity at all, not even in the brain stem. Without the aid of machinery, such patients are unable to breathe, and their hearts are unable to beat. PVS patients, by contrast, have a functioning brain stem. They don't, however, have any awareness of themselves or of the world around them. This makes PVS patients different from minimally conscious patients, who have at least some awareness at least some of the time.

Sometimes a PVS patient improves, but, if improvement occurs, it usually does so within the first three months. After six months, PVS patients almost never regain even minimal consciousness, but remain vegetative for the rest of their lives. Such patients can't eat or drink on their own; they must be fed through a gastric tube surgically implanted in their stomachs, and they must be hydrated through an IV line. Because they easily get infections, they must be given IV antibiotics prophylactically. They must also lie on special mattresses and be periodically moved to prevent bedsores. Some PVS patients live like this for decades.

This is the future that Terri faces.

June 18, 1990

Michael is appointed Terri's guardian. Terri's parents, Robert and Mary Schindler, don't object. The Schindlers get along well with Michael. In fact, Michael is now living with the Schindlers in the Schindlers' home, also in St. Petersburg, Florida.

June 1990 to February 1993

Michael aggressively pursues a variety of treatments for his wife. For example, in November 1990 he takes Terri to California for experimental "brain stimulator" treatment, and in July 1991 he transfers Terri to Sable Palms, a skilled care facility in Florida, where she receives ongoing neurological testing and speech/occupational therapy. If he doesn't like something her care providers are doing, he doesn't hesitate to express his concerns. Despite all that he does for her, however, Terri's condition shows no improvement.

In November 1992 Michael sues the gynecologists Terri had before she collapsed. His argument is that the gynecologists failed to detect the potassium imbalance that resulted in Terri's heart attack, which in turn led to Terri's brain damage. Michael wins the lawsuit. He is awarded $750,000 for Terri's ongoing care and an additional $300,000 for his loss and suffering.

1993

In February Michael has a falling out with the Schindlers. The Schindlers claim they are concerned about the course of therapy that Michael is providing for their daughter. In July the Schindlers sue Michael, asking the court that they be allowed to replace Michael as Terri's legal guardians. The lawsuit is eventually dismissed. Michael claims that the dispute is really over the $300,000 that he was awarded the previous year, that the Schindlers are trying to force him to share the money with them.

1994

Michael asks his wife's doctors how likely it is that she'll ever regain consciousness. When the doctors tell him that this is extremely unlikely, Michael asks that his wife not be resuscitated if she suffers a heart attack or if some other life-threatening event occurs. Michael also begins a relationship with Jodi Centonze, and later has two children with her. Michael's relationship with the Schindlers continues to deteriorate.

1998 to 2000

In May 1998 Michael petitions the Circuit Court for Pinellas County in Florida to allow him to remove the gastric tube that feeds Terri so that she can die. He admits that Terri left no written instructions, but he claims that on several occasions she told him that she would not want to live in a vegetative state with no chance of recovery. A handful of Terri's acquaintances make similar claims, but the Schindlers disagree. They argue that they raised their daughter as a Roman Catholic, that Roman Catholicism opposes ending the lives of PVS patients, and that consequently their daughter would not want her feeding tube removed.

On December 29, 1999, Richard Pearse, the court-appointed guardian ad litem – or person advocating for the best interests of Terri – issues his report. In his report Pearse expresses his suspicion that, by seeking to remove his wife's feeding tube, Michael may be thinking more about his own interests than those of his wife. The basis of the suspicion is that, if his wife were to die, he, as the husband, would inherit the entirety of her estate. Pearse suggests that this might explain why Michael has opted not to divorce his wife and marry Ms. Centonze – if he were to do that, the Schindlers would be the ones to inherit Terri's estate.

Despite Pearse's suspicions, on February 11, 2000, George Greer, the presiding judge for the Circuit Court for Pinellas County, rules that Michael may remove his wife's feeding tube. Greer argues that Michael's motivations are irrelevant, that the only relevant issues at hand are 1) whether Terri has any chance of improving and 2) what Terri would want. According to Terri's doctors, the answer to the first question is "No," and, as for the second question, Judge Greer sees sufficient evidence that Terri would not want to live the rest of her life in a vegetative state. The Schindlers, who, contrary to what the medical experts claim, believe that their daughter has a chance of regaining consciousness, appeal Judge Greer's decision.

April 2001

On April 24, after all appeals have been exhausted and the U.S. Supreme Court has declined to review the case, Terri's feeding tube is removed. Two days later the Schindlers sue Michael on the grounds that he committed perjury when he stated that his wife wouldn't want to live in a vegetative state with no chance of recovery. The courts order that Terri's feeding tube be reinserted until this new lawsuit comes to a conclusion.

2001 to 2003

The Schindlers continue their legal maneuvers to block the removal of their daughter's feeding tube, and they enlist the support of prolife groups and conservative Christians. In violation of a court order, they release a videotape of Terri that convinces many viewers that she has some cognitive abilities. They repeatedly accuse Michael of abuse, claiming that he is neglecting Terri's hygiene, denying her dental care, poisoning her, and physically harming her. The Florida Department of Children and Families investigates all the charges but finds no evidence of abuse. The Schindlers also claim that Terri never had a heart attack, but instead that Michael strangled her but failed to kill her, and that's how she ended up in a vegetative state. All of these maneuvers, however, ultimately fail.

October 2003

On October 15, Terri's feeding tube is removed for the second time. In response the Florida state legislature passes "Terri's Law," allowing Governor Jeb Bush, brother of President George W. Bush, to order that the feeding tube be replaced. Governor Bush issues the order on October 21.

2004

In September the Florida Supreme Court rules that "Terri's Law" is unconstitutional. The reason the law is unconstitutional is that it violates the separation of powers – that is, by passing "Terri's Law," the Florida legislature attempted to do what only the courts are allowed to do. In October Governor Bush says he will file a petition with the U.S. Supreme Court.

January 2005

The U.S. Supreme Court refuses to review the case.

March 18, 2005

For the third time Terri's feeding tube is removed.

March 21, 2005

The U.S. Senate and House of Representatives pass the Palm Sunday Compromise, and President George W. Bush signs it. The Palm Sunday Compromise is an attempt to save Terri's life by allowing the federal courts to hear the case: "The United States District Court for the Middle District of Florida shall have jurisdiction to hear, determine, and render judgment on a suit or claim by or on behalf of Theresa Marie Schiavo for the alleged violation of any right of Theresa Marie Schiavo under the Constitution or laws of the United States relating to the withholding or withdrawal of food, fluids, or medical treatment necessary to sustain her life."

March 22, 2005

The United States District Court for the Middle District of Florida refuses to order the reinsertion of Terri's feeding tube.

March 31, 2005

Protesters stand outside Woodside Hospice, where Terri is a patient. Many of them carry signs. The messages on the signs convey anger:

"Murder Is Legal in America," "Hospice or Auschwitz," "Hey, Judge, Who Made You God?" Inside the hospice, cradling Terri's head, is Michael. Shortly after 9:00 a.m., Terri stops breathing – she dies as a result of dehydration. The Schindlers are not present – at Michael's request.

April 1, 2005

Terri's body is cremated, after an extensive autopsy has been conducted.

June 15, 2005

The results of the autopsy are made public. The original diagnosis of PVS was correct. Because of the lack of oxygen caused by the cardiac arrest, Terri's brain shrank to less than half its normal weight. Terri would never have regained even minimal cognitive functioning, no matter what treatment the doctors prescribed.

The autopsy reveals no signs of strangulation or abuse. It also reveals no evidence of a heart attack. According to the report, Terri had a potassium imbalance, but the imbalance was discovered only after the doctors at the hospital had given her several drugs known to lower potassium in the blood. This casts doubt on the claim that a potassium imbalance caused Terri's cardiac arrest, as well as on the claim that Terri suffered from bulimia. As the autopsy report states, "No one observed [Terri] taking diet pills, binging and purging or consuming laxatives, and she apparently never confessed to her family or friends about having an eating disorder."

What, then, caused Terri's cardiac arrest? No one knows. The autopsy report concludes, "The manner of death will therefore be certified as undetermined."

January 2006

Michael marries Jodi Centonze. The couple and their two children continue to live in Florida.

Questions for reflection: Should Michael have sought to remove Terri's feeding tube? Should the Schindlers have tried to block Michael's efforts? Did the courts make appropriate rulings? Should Terri have been allowed to die?

Puzzle 11
A Tale of Two Cities

NEW YORK – September 11, 2001

7:59 AM. American Airlines Flight 11 takes off at Boston's Logan International Airport. The plane is a Boeing 767 bound for Los Angeles. On board are ninety-two passengers and crew. Among the passengers are Mohamed Atta of Egypt, who received flight training in the U.S., and four Saudis – Abdulaziz al-Omari, Wail al-Shehri, Waleed al-Shehri, and Satam al-Suqami. All five of these men have ties with Al Qaeda.

8:14 AM. A second Boeing 767 bound for Los Angeles, United Airlines Flight 175, takes off from Logan. Sixty-five passengers and crew are on board, including five more men who have ties with Al Qaeda: Marwan al-Shehhi and Fayez Banihammad of the United Arab Emirates, and Mohand al-Shehri, Hamza al-Ghamdi, and Ahmed al-Ghamdi, each from Saudi Arabia. Like Mohamed Atta on Flight 11, Marwan al-Shehhi received flight training in the U.S.

8:19 AM. Betty Ong and Madeline Amy Sweeney, flight attendants on Flight 11, call the American Airlines operation center from an airphone in economy class, and for the next twenty-five minutes report what they see. Ong says, "The cockpit is not answering the phone. There is somebody stabbed in business class. They can't breathe in business class. They've got Mace or something. I don't know, but I think we're getting hijacked."

8:24 AM. Mohamed Atta sends a message from Flight 11: "We have some planes. Just stay quiet and you'll be okay. We are returning to the airport." A minute later, he adds, "Nobody move. Everything will be okay. If you try to make any moves, you'll endanger yourself and the airplane. Just stay quiet." The message is presumably meant for the passengers aboard Flight 11 but is transmitted to ground control at Logan by accident. The passengers never hear the message.

8:34 AM. Atta sends a second message to ground control, also presumably intended for the passengers: "Nobody move please. We are going back to the airport. Don't try to make any stupid moves." As before, the passengers don't hear the message.

8:40 AM. The Northeast Air Defense Sector orders two fighter planes to find and follow Flight 11. The fighter planes are on Cape Cod, at Otis Air National Guard Base.

8:44 AM. Still on the phone with the American Airlines operation center, flight attendant Sweeney says, "I see water. I see buildings. We are flying low. We are flying very, very low. We are flying way too low. Oh my God, we are flying way too low. Oh my god!" This is the last message that comes from Flight 11.

8:46 AM. Flight 11 crashes into floors 93-99 of the North Tower of the World Trade Center in Manhattan. Hundreds of people in the North Tower are killed, as is everyone on board Flight 11. The two fighter planes sent to find and follow Flight 11 haven't yet taken off from Cape Cod.

8:52 AM. Peter Hanson, a passenger aboard Flight 175, calls his father: "I think they've taken over the cockpit. An attendant has been stabbed and someone else up front may have been killed. The plane is making strange moves. Call United Airlines."

9:00 AM. Hanson calls his father again: "It's getting bad, Dad. A stewardess was stabbed. They seem to have knives and Mace. They said they have a bomb. Passengers are throwing up and getting sick. The plane is making jerky movements. I don't think the pilot is flying the plane. I think we are going down. I think they intend to go to Chicago or someplace and fly into a building. Don't worry, Dad. If it happens, it'll be very fast. My God, my God."

9:03 AM. Hanson's father, having turned on the television, sees Flight 175 crash into floors 75-85 of the World Trade Center's South Tower. Hundreds of people in the South Tower are killed, as is everyone on board Flight 175.

9:59 AM. The South Tower collapses.

10:28 AM. The North Tower collapses.

8:30 PM. President George W. Bush addresses the nation. He labels the morning's events "evil, despicable acts of terror" and promises that the U.S. and its allies will "win the war against terrorism." The death toll at the World Trade Center is eventually set at 2,753, and the overall death toll – including the victims at the Pentagon, the passengers and crew aboard the four planes that crashed, and the nineteen perpetrators of the attacks – is 2,996.

On December 27, 2001, Al Jazeera, an Arabic news network based in Qatar, airs a thirty-three-minute videotape in which Osama bin

Laden praises the attacks of 9/11. In defense of the attacks, bin Laden makes several claims.

First, the attacks served as retribution against the U.S. for its acts of terrorism against Muslims: "The United States is practicing the detestable terrorism in its ugliest forms in Palestine and Iraq. Bush the father – the ill-famed man – was the reason behind the killing of over one million children in Iraq. This is in addition to the men and women. What happened on 11 September is nothing but a reaction to the continuing injustice being done to our children in Palestine, Iraq, Somalia, southern Sudan, and elsewhere, as well as Kashmir and Asia."

Second, the attacks will help put an end to the oppression of Muslims by the West; third, the attacks were a form of self-defense; fourth, the attacks were in accordance with the will of God: "Our terrorism against America is commendable. It seeks to make the unjust stop making injustice. It seeks to make America stop its support for Israel, which kills our people. The issue is very clear, cannot you be reasonable? America and the Western leaders repeatedly said that Hamas and the Islamic Jihad in Palestine and other warring organizations are terrorism organizations. If self-defense is terrorism, what is legitimate then? Our defense and our fighting are not different from the fighting of our brothers in Palestine, such as Hamas. We fight for the sake of Almighty God and to make the word of God the higher word and the word of the unbelievers the lower one, and to end the oppression inflicted on the weak in Palestine and elsewhere."

Finally, the nineteen perpetrators of the attacks will be rewarded in the afterlife: "No Muslim would in any case wonder what was gained by the perpetrators of the September 11th attacks or say that they wasted their lives, and whoever says so is a complete ignoramus. They won the satisfaction of God the Almighty and the heaven God promised them. For victory is not only material gains, but also adherence to principles."

HIROSHIMA – August 6, 1945

1:45 AM.[3] A Boeing B-29, with the words *Enola Gay* painted on its nose, takes off from North Field on Tinian, an island located in the

---

[3] All times listed are local times in Hiroshima. Tinian, in a different time zone, is one hour ahead of Hiroshima. Thus, the *Enola Gay* began its mission at 2:45 Tinian time.

Pacific Ocean. The aircraft carries an atomic bomb, dubbed Little Boy, which has the explosive power of 16,000 tons of TNT. The plan is to drop the bomb on Hiroshima, a six-hour flight from Tinian, but Kokura and Nagasaki are designated alternative targets, in case conditions at Hiroshima prove unsatisfactory. The pilot is Lieutenant Colonel Paul Tibbets. Accompanying the *Enola Gay* are *The Great Artiste*, which carries instrumentation to measure the blast, and an aircraft later named *Necessary Evil*, which will take photographs to record the bombing.

4:55 AM. After flying separately, the *Enola Gay*, *The Great Artiste*, and *Necessary Evil* rendezvous at Iwo Jima, an island lying between Tinian and Japan. From here, they fly together toward Hiroshima.

6:30 AM. Captain William "Deak" Parsons arms the bomb. About an hour later, his assistant, Second Lieutenant Morris Jeppson removes the safety devices.

7:00 AM. An air raid alert is sounded in Hiroshima when the Japanese detect an American plane, *Straight Flush*, flying overhead. *Straight Flush*, however, doesn't drop any bombs. It's there only to provide a weather report. It sends a message to the *Enola Gay*: "Cloud cover less than 3/10th at all altitudes. Advice: bomb primary."

7:09 AM. As *Straight Flush* departs, the air raid alert ends.

8:09 AM. Having arrived at Hiroshima, Tibbets starts the *Enola Gay*'s bombing run at an altitude of 9,400 meters, and then hands over controls to his bombardier Major Thomas Ferebee.

8:15 AM. Ferebee releases the bomb, aiming for the Aioi Bridge. Little Boy takes 44.4 seconds to fall from 9,400 meters to 580 meters above Hiroshima, where it detonates. Because of crosswinds, however, the bomb drifts 800 meters from the intended target of the Aioi Bridge, detonating directly above Shima Surgical Clinic. The bomb carves out a swath of complete destruction having a radius measuring 1.6 kilometers, and sets off a firestorm spreading over eleven square kilometers. Between 70,000 and 80,000 people – 50,000 or 60,000 of them civilians and about 20,000 of them soldiers – die from the blast or the fires, and as many more are injured. As the weeks and months pass, the death toll rises to somewhere between 90,000 and 166,000. Just before the bomb detonated, Hiroshima had a population of approximately 340,000-350,000.

8:16 AM. Two shockwaves from the blast, the first stronger than the second, reach the *Enola Gay*, now 18.5 kilometers from ground zero. The *Enola Gay* is buffeted about, but sustains no damage.

1:58 PM. The *Enola Gay* returns to Tinian without incident. Upon landing, Paul Tibbets is awarded the Distinguished Service Cross.

On August 9, 1945, in a radio address to the American people, President Harry S. Truman defends the development and use of the atomic bomb. In the course of his speech, he advances several arguments:

1. Japan brought the bombing on itself, by refusing to accept the terms of unconditional surrender set forth in the Potsdam Declaration.
2. Hiroshima was a military base, and thus bombing it spared civilians as much as possible.
3. If the U.S. hadn't developed the atomic bomb first, its enemies might have, with disastrous results.
4. The Japanese committed numerous atrocities against Americans.
5. Use of the atomic bomb might shorten the war and save countless American lives.
6. Properly used, the atomic bomb can secure world peace.
7. Properly used, the atomic bomb can serve God's purposes.

The relevant portion of Truman's speech is this:

"The British, Chinese, and United States Governments have given the Japanese people adequate warning of what is in store for them. We have laid down the general terms on which they can surrender. Our warning went unheeded; our terms were rejected. Since then the Japanese have seen what our atomic bomb can do. They can foresee what it will do in the future.

"The world will note that the first atomic bomb was dropped on Hiroshima, a military base. That was because we wished in this first attack to avoid, insofar as possible, the killing of civilians. But that attack is only a warning of things to come. If Japan does not surrender, bombs will have to be dropped on her war industries and, unfortunately, thousands of civilian lives will be lost. I urge Japanese civilians to leave industrial cities immediately, and save themselves from destruction.

"I realize the tragic significance of the atomic bomb.

"Its production and its use were not lightly undertaken by this Government. But we knew that our enemies were on the search for it. We know now how close they were to finding it. And we knew the disaster which would come to this Nation, and to all peace-loving nations, to all civilization, if they had found it first.

"That is why we felt compelled to undertake the long and uncertain and costly labor of discovery and production.

"We won the race of discovery against the Germans.

"Having found the bomb we have used it. We have used it against those who attacked us without warning at Pearl Harbor, against those who have starved and beaten and executed American prisoners of war, against those who have abandoned all pretense of obeying international laws of warfare. We have used it in order to shorten the agony of war, in order to save the lives of thousands and thousands of young Americans.

"We shall continue to use it until we completely destroy Japan's power to make war. Only a Japanese surrender will stop us.

"The atomic bomb is too dangerous to be loose in a lawless world. That is why Great Britain, Canada, and the United States, who have the secret of its production, do not intend to reveal that secret until means have been found to control the bomb so as to protect ourselves and the rest of the world from the danger of total destruction.

"As far back as last May, Secretary of War Stimson, at my suggestion, appointed a committee upon which Secretary of State Byrnes served as my personal representative, to prepare plans for the future control of this bomb. I shall ask the Congress to cooperate to the end that its production and use be controlled, and that its power be made an overwhelming influence towards world peace.

"We must constitute ourselves trustees of this new force – to prevent its misuse, and to turn it into the channels of service to mankind.

"It is an awful responsibility which has come to us.

"We thank God that it has come to us, instead of to our enemies; and we pray that He may guide us to use it in His ways and for His purposes."

Questions for reflection: What is terrorism? Were 9/11 and the use of the atomic bomb on Hiroshima both terrorist acts? Was one morally worse than the other? Did both violate people's right to life? Can terrorism ever be justified? Are Osama bin Laden's arguments in defense of 9/11 convincing? Are Harry S. Truman's arguments in defense of the use of the atomic bomb on Hiroshima convincing?

Puzzle 12
"You Are Causing Aggression to Us"

Lunch in hand, G. W. seats himself at an unoccupied table, picking up the newspaper that some earlier customer has abandoned and tossing it onto a neighboring table. As the paper lands, the pages flutter open to a grease-stained editorial. The editorial blasts the U.S. government, and U.S. citizens, for failing to do what's necessary to curb global warming. All too many Americans, the editorial says, are self-absorbed, obsessed with profit and material possessions, showing little concern for the health of the environment. G. W. doesn't read the editorial. Instead, he checks his email while gobbling down his bacon double cheeseburger and soda. This is what he typically eats during his lunch break. It's cheap, it's quick – and it's an ingrained habit. The habit has its origins in his childhood, when the centerpiece of every meal his family ate was some kind of meat ...

In 2007 the president of Uganda, Yoweri Museveni, delivered a speech at an African Union summit. Referring to people living in the wealthy countries of Europe and North America, he said, "You are causing aggression to us by causing global warming." President Museveni's statement caused a stir. Especially troubling was the word "aggression," which conjures up images of terrorist bombings, murders, and armed robberies. People who commit such acts are evil, intentionally harming others, intentionally violating the rights of others. How different from these people do the overwhelming majority of the citizens of wealthy countries seem! They're only minding their own business, pursuing their interests, spending their hard-earned money as they see fit. They don't mean to hurt anyone. Accusing them of causing aggression seems ludicrous – even shocking.

Yet President Museveni's statement shouldn't be casually dismissed, for embedded within it are four claims that deserve careful consideration:

1. Global warming is occurring.
2. Among the chief causes of global warming is the behavior of people who live in wealthy countries.

3. Among the chief effects of global warming is harm to those who contribute to global warming the least – the people who live in developing countries.
4. Behavior that contributes to global warming is a serious moral wrong.

... Slurping up the last of his soda, G. W. steps out into the sweltering parking lot, hops in his Ford Explorer, and cranks up the A/C. The car needs gas, so he stops at the gas station next door. Grumbling, he swears that half his paycheck is spent on gasoline, but it's his own fault. He could have bought a more fuel-efficient vehicle, and he could have chosen to live closer to his workplace, where he wouldn't have to deal with an hour commute each way. He could often also walk rather than drive. The Burger King where he just finished his lunch, for example, is only three blocks from his workplace, yet he never walks there. Driving is another of G. W.'s ingrained habits ...

1. Is global warming occurring? Donald Trump, who in June 2017 withdrew the U.S. from the Paris climate accord, an international agreement that aims to limit the rise in global temperature to less than 2° C above preindustrial levels, occasionally questions the reality of global warming in a tweet. For example, on January 29, 2014, Trump tweeted, "Snowing in Texas and Louisiana, record setting freezing temperatures throughout the country and beyond. Global warming is an expensive hoax!" Millions of Americans – mostly conservative Republicans – share Trump's skepticism.

With this skepticism, however, climate scientists – who have much greater expertise on questions of global warming than either Trump or ordinary Americans, whether they be conservative Republicans or liberal Democrats – overwhelmingly disagree. According to NASA, ninety-seven percent of actively publishing climate scientists affirm that global warming is a fact. The Intergovernmental Panel on Climate Change (IPCC), the leading international body that studies global warming, sums up the prevailing view: "Scientific evidence for warming of the climate system is unequivocal, as is now evident from observations of increases in average global air and ocean temperatures, widespread melting of snow and ice, and rising global average sea level."

Since 1880, when measurements were first taken, the average global temperature has increased by about 1.9° F, with nine of the ten warmest years on record being in the twenty-first century – the exception is 1998 – and the warmest year of all being 2016. Although seemingly small, this temperature increase has resulted in significant melting of glaciers and polar ice caps. For instance, Greenland loses 270 billion tons of its ice sheet each year, and the volume of summer ice floating on the Arctic Ocean has decreased markedly since the late 1970s, when accurate satellite measurements became available – the volume of ice in 2011, for example, was only a quarter of what it was in 1979. With all this melting of snow and ice, sea levels have risen – about seventeen centimeters in the last hundred years.

What, then, of Donald Trump's observation of snow in Texas and Louisiana, and record cold temperatures? As it turns out, one of the effects of global warming is that the jet stream becomes loopier, with arctic air occasionally dipping farther south than it normally does. Thus, some parts of the world will sometimes be colder than normal – because of global warming! To determine whether global warming is real, we shouldn't focus on just one part of the world at just one time, as Trump did, but look at the whole globe over a period of many years. When we do that, we find powerful evidence of global warming, and we find that globally the year 2014, the year Trump sent his tweet, was at the time the warmest year on record, and is now the fifth warmest, behind 2015, 2016, 2017, and 2018.

Of the four claims embedded in President Museveni's statement, the first is far more likely true than false.

... G. W. climbs back into his car and drives the three blocks to his workplace. Although his job can get monotonous – like most of his friends, he spends his day in a cubicle – the pay is decent enough to allow him to travel whenever he accumulates some vacation time. He's been to eleven countries, and every continent except Antarctica. In another three months, he'll fly to Paris for a week. Paris is one of his favorite destinations – he's been there twice before ...

2. What are the causes of global warming? Ice cores taken from Antarctica reveal that for at least the last 650,000 years the Earth has cycled regularly between ice ages and warmer periods. These epochal cycles have occurred because of slight changes in the Earth's orbit around the sun, not because of anything human beings have done. In contrast, according to climate scientists, who are once again in overwhelming agreement, the warming that has taken place only very recently, during the last century and a half, ever since the Industrial Revolution, is the result of human activity.

Human beings cause global warming by emitting greenhouse gases – such as carbon dioxide and methane – into the atmosphere. For the ten thousand years preceding the Industrial Revolution and going back to the end of the last ice age, the concentration of carbon dioxide in the atmosphere was a steady 275 parts per million (ppm), while the concentration of methane was a steady 700 parts per billion (ppb). Today, because of human activity, the concentrations of these gases have risen to 412 ppm and 1,866 ppb, respectively. These gases can remain in the atmosphere for centuries, warming the earth by acting as a blanket, preventing heat from escaping into outer space. Human beings do many things that emit greenhouse gases, including the following:

- Burning fossil fuels. The hour that G. W. commutes, the three blocks he drives to the Burger King, and the flights he takes overseas all involve the burning of fossil fuels, and all contribute to global warming.
- Eating meat, especially beef. As cows digest their feed, they produce great quantities of methane, a particularly powerful greenhouse gas, which they belch into the atmosphere. In the United States alone, between thirty and forty million cows are reared and slaughtered each year. The meat industry, supported by the dietary habits of people like G. W., is a significant contributor to global warming.
- Cutting down trees. Trees remove carbon dioxide from the atmosphere by making the carbon a part of their bodies. When land is deforested, the carbon from the bodies of the felled and decaying trees returns to the atmosphere. Cutting down trees to produce paper, such as the newspaper G. W. tosses onto a neighboring table at the Burger King, contributes to global warming, as does cutting down trees to provide space for the animals people consume.

Human activities such as these also generate feedback loops that result in yet further warming of the Earth. For example, as people burn fossil fuels, eat meat, and cut down trees, the permafrost in the Arctic – a layer of soil that normally remains frozen throughout the year – begins to thaw. As it thaws, massive quantities of methane, which for millennia have been trapped underneath the permafrost, bubble to the surface and escape into the atmosphere, adding to the greenhouse effect. Similarly, as the Arctic ice cap melts, more of the sun's rays strike ocean water rather than ice. Since ocean water is darker than ice, it doesn't reflect the sun's rays back into outer space, as ice does, but instead absorbs the sun's rays, causing increased warming.

For the most part, the people who contribute to global warming, people like G. W., live in wealthy countries. The U.S., Canada, and Australia, among the biggest contributors per capita, each emit more than fifteen tons of carbon dioxide per person per year. Germany comes in at 8.9 tons, China at 7.5, India at 1.7, and Sri Lanka at 0.9. The emissions of some poor countries, including many of those in sub-Saharan Africa, are negligible. Uganda, for example, President Museveni's home country, emits only 0.1 tons of carbon dioxide per person per year. According to one (possibly overly optimistic) estimate, global warming could be kept under control if each person in the world emitted no more than two tons of carbon dioxide per year. If this is correct, Americans are emitting far more than their share.

Thus, like the first of the four claims embedded in President Museveni's statement, the second – that among the chief causes of global warming is the behavior of people who live in wealthy countries – is backed by a wealth of evidence. As time has passed, that evidence has strengthened rather than weakened.

... Settling down in his cubicle, G. W. gets back to work. He's preparing a PowerPoint presentation that he has to deliver tomorrow. It occurs to him that his audience might more easily follow his presentation, and take notes, if he gives them hard copies of his PowerPoint slides, so he heads to the photocopier, making several extra copies in case his audience is larger than he expects – better to be safe than sorry. The photocopier spits out a full ream of paper etched with his PowerPoint slides. As he lugs all those copies back to his cubicle, he chuckles to himself, thinking, "I'm glad I'm not the one who pays for the paper!" ...

3. What are the effects of global warming? The Swedish scientist Svante Arrhenius, who in 1896 was the first to speculate that industrialization causes global warming, believed that global warming would be beneficial, stimulating the production of food. Scientists today, however, overwhelmingly reject Arrhenius' optimism. Current evidence suggests that among the effects of global warming are these:

- An increase in violent weather, such as Category 5 hurricanes.

- Desertification of some parts of the world, including much of Australia and Africa.
- Flooding of coastal cities and low-lying Pacific island nations, caused by rising sea levels.
- Acidification of the oceans, which, killing shellfish by preventing them from forming sufficiently thick shells, adversely impacts the fishing industry.
- The spread of diseases, such as malaria and diarrhea.

The poorest nations are the ones that suffer the most, because they lack the resources to respond to threats like these. The Netherlands, for instance, a low-lying country threatened by rising sea levels, has enough wealth that it was able to install raised dykes, and is capable of building houses that, while attached to the ground, can rise and float in times of flooding. By contrast, in India, where millions of people live in low-lying coastal regions, funding for high-tech solutions such as these is unavailable. As a result, hundreds of Indian families have been displaced from their homes, and, as sea levels continue to rise, the number of displaced families will only increase.

According to the World Health Organization (WHO), the impact of global warming is already serious, and it will get worse. It estimates that about 150,000 people currently die each year from causes related to global warming, and that between the years 2030 and 2050 this number will rise to about 250,000. Most of these people are from poor countries. For instance, in Uganda, President Museveni's home country, between eighty and one hundred twenty climate-change deaths per million people already occurred in 2000. This contrasts with the United States, Canada, and Australia, among the biggest emitters of greenhouse gases per person, where a mere zero to two climate-change deaths per million people occurred in 2000.

All this suggests that also true is the third of the four claims implicit in President Museveni's statement – that among the chief effects of global warming is harm to those who contribute to global warming the least.

... G. W. puts on the sweater he keeps tucked away in his cubicle. During the summer, the building is always chilly – too much A/C. G. W.'s house, though, isn't much better. During the summer, he keeps the thermostat set at a cool 20° C even when he's not at home. This may seem to be a waste of energy, but, when he comes home, he doesn't want to have to turn on the A/C and then wait fifteen

minutes for the house to cool. He wants his house to be cool the moment he opens the door. He could, of course, use the timer to set the A/C to turn on, say, at 6:00 p.m., but he doesn't bother because he never knows exactly when he'll get home – sometimes he can sneak out of the office a few minutes early and sometimes rush hour traffic is lighter than he expects ...

4. Is behavior that contributes to global warming a serious moral wrong? If 150,000 people die each year because of global warming, it would seem that behavior that contributes to global warming must be very wrong indeed. G. W. and people like him, it would seem, must have a powerful moral obligation to reduce their greenhouse gas emissions from twenty tons of carbon dioxide a year to no more than two tons a year – and to do this they must burn much less fossil fuel, eat much less meat, and use much less paper and other products made from trees. Against this view, however, G. W. and people like him might advance a number of arguments.

First, they might plead ignorance, arguing that they didn't know they're harming anyone, and that consequently they're not responsible for the harm they cause. This argument, however, faces the objection that, even if they're not aware of the harm they cause, they ought to be aware. Information about global warming and its harmful effects is easily available, so that those who choose not to educate themselves are negligent. In this respect, G. W. and people like him are similar to drivers who are pulled over for speeding and who, despite the clearly marked speed limit signs, say in their defense, "But I didn't know I was speeding!" Speeding motorists ought to know the speed limit, and they deserve the speeding tickets they get.

Second, G. W. might argue that he has obligations primarily to himself and those near to him – family, friends, and, to a lesser extent, acquaintances and fellow countrymen. Toward strangers living in distant lands, such as Africa, his obligations are negligible at best. This is the argument that George W. Bush articulated early in his presidency. In 2001, when he was asked about global warming, Bush stated, "We will not do anything that harms our economy, because first things first are the people who live in America." Donald Trump espouses a similar view when he supports an "America first" approach to international affairs. In response to this, critics accuse Bush and Trump of flagrant chauvinism. Surely Americans don't count so much more than people of other nations that they may cause the deaths of thousands of people a year.

Third, G. W. might defend himself on the grounds that, even if the wealthy nations collectively cause 150,000 people to die each year, it's far from certain that G. W. by himself causes harm to anyone. So he emits twenty tons of carbon dioxide a year, perhaps 1,600 tons in his lifetime. How much harm can that cause? According to the World Health Organization, a great deal: emitting just 800 tons of carbon dioxide in a lifetime – half of what G. W. emits – will decrease healthy human life on this planet by more than six months. Those six months may be spread out across a large number of people – perhaps millions or billions of them – so that no one person is affected by more than a few seconds, but the aggregate decrease in healthy human life is significant.

Fourth, even if – G. W. might say – he himself causes harm by his emissions, there's no way of knowing which specific individuals are harmed. The victims are unidentifiable. This contrasts with, say, the murder of one's neighbor, gunned down in broad daylight, in which case one knows who the victim is. But what does it matter whether the victims are identifiable? Whether they're identifiable or not, the consequences are the same – namely, in both cases, people die. Suppose, for example, that G. W. is a traveling salesman, selling cans of tuna. Suppose further that he knows the tuna is tainted and that some people who eat the tuna will get sick, but he doesn't know which specific individuals will get sick and which won't. The victims are unidentifiable, but wouldn't G. W. still do something very wrong if he sells the tuna he knows is tainted?

Finally, G. W. might argue that he isn't doing anything wrong because, even if he foresees that his emissions harm others, he doesn't intend any harm. It's not as if he wants anyone to get malaria or starve to death because of a drought brought on by global warming. All he wants is a convenient meal at Burger King and a pleasantly air-conditioned house. But it's not clear that this defense works either. Foreseen but unintended harms are at least sometimes impermissible. Thus, suppose that a man knows he has an STD but engages in unprotected sex anyway. He foresees that his partner may be harmed, but he may not intend the harm. He may intend only to experience the pleasure of sex. Nonetheless, by engaging in unprotected sex, he does something seriously wrong. What about the unintended harms that G. W. causes? Are they among the unintended harms that are impermissible, or might they be permissible? Perhaps they'd be permissible if the harms were outweighed by some greater good. But whatever good results from G. W.'s behavior – for example, the convenience of not waiting fifteen minutes for his house to cool when he comes home from work – seems trivial by comparison to the loss of life caused by global warming. In these circumstances, the unintended harms that G. W. causes seem impermissible.

In light of all these considerations, President Museveni's statement – that people in wealthy nations cause aggression to people in poor nations – may not be so farfetched. Perhaps it's even true. Perhaps people like G. W. are violating the rights of many thousands of the poorest, most vulnerable people on the planet.

G. W. sits in a café in Paris, sipping a martini. His face beams contentment – not the slightest twinge of guilt tugs at his soul. Why should it? Life is good.

Questions for reflection: Do people in wealthy nations cause aggression to people living in poor nations by causing global warming? Are the rights of people who are harmed by global warming violated? To help curb global warming, should G. W. burn less fossil fuel, eat less meat, and use less paper and other products made from trees? What's the best way to approach the problem of global warming?

Puzzle 13
Desecration of the Flag

Street v. New York

On June 6, 1966, while he was in his Brooklyn apartment, Sydney Street heard on the radio that James Meredith, a prominent civil rights leader, had been shot by a sniper in Mississippi. Outraged, Street said to himself, "They didn't protect him." He opened a drawer and took out a neatly folded American flag, which he used to display on national holidays. It was an older flag, made when the United States consisted of only forty-eight states, and so it showed only forty-eight stars. Street left his apartment with the flag still neatly folded, and proceeded to the nearby intersection of St. James Place and Lafayette Avenue. Standing on the northeast corner of the intersection, Street struck a match and then set his flag on fire. He dropped the burning flag onto the pavement.

As the flag was burning, a police officer passed by in his cruiser. Stepping out to investigate, the officer saw about thirty people standing near the burning flag on the northeast corner of the intersection, and on the northwest corner another five or ten people, including Street, who was "talking out loud" to the others. As the officer approached, he overheard Street say, "We don't need no damn flag." When he asked Street if he was the one who burned the flag, Street answered, "Yes, that is my flag. I burned it. If they let that happen to Meredith, we don't need an American flag."

Later that day, Street was charged with malicious mischief, having cast contempt upon the American flag, and eventually was found guilty and given a suspended sentence. Street appealed his verdict all the way to the United States Supreme Court. By a margin of 5-4, the Court overturned the verdict, upholding Street's First Amendment right to freedom of speech.

Radich v. New York

On December 27, 1966, a police officer passed by Stephen Radich's art gallery on Madison Avenue in Manhattan. Displayed in the gallery's second-floor window was an American flag stuffed in the vague shape of a human being hanging from a yellow noose. The next day the officer returned with a police photographer, went inside the gallery, and saw on exhibit thirteen constructions featuring the American and other flags. The flag hanging from the noose was still there, as was an American flag wrapped around an object shaped like a gun caisson. Also on exhibit was a cross, seven feet tall, "with a bishop's mitre on the head-piece, the arms wrapped in ecclesiastical flags and an erect penis wrapped in an American flag protruding from the vertical standard." The police officer served Radich with a criminal summons, on the grounds that, by displaying the constructions, Radich was casting contempt upon the American flag.

The constructions were all created by artist Marc Morrel, a former Marine, who intended the works as a protest against the Vietnam War and war in general. At his trial, Radich testified that he shared Morrel's opposition to the war in Vietnam and that, to accentuate the antiwar sentiments expressed by Morrel's constructions, he placed a tape recorder in his gallery that played antiwar music by protest singer Phil Ochs. He claimed that he did not intend any disrespect to the American flag. Also testifying at Radich's trial was Hilton Kramer, the art news editor of *The New York Times*, who stated that, by contemporary standards, Morrel's pieces all qualified as works of art. No one testified that Morrel's pieces caused any disorder or disturbance.

Radich was found guilty and ordered to pay a $500 fine or serve sixty days in jail. Radich appealed the verdict, and the case eventually made its way to the United States Supreme Court. The Supreme Court, however, was equally divided in its opinion, four justices supporting the verdict and four justices opposed. Because the Court was equally divided, Radich was permitted to turn for a final decision to a federal district court. The federal district court reversed Radich's conviction.

Smith v. Goguen

On January 30, 1970, a police officer accosted Valarie Goguen on a public street in Leominster, Massachusetts. Goguen was with a group of people, standing and talking together. The group wasn't engaging in any public demonstration or protest, nor was it disrupting traffic or otherwise disturbing the peace. Goguen, however, was wearing a small American flag, about four inches by six inches, sewn into the left side of the rear end of his blue jeans. When the police officer asked Goguen about the flag, the group of people Goguen was with laughed. Later the same day, a second police officer, seeing Goguen walking through the business district of Leominster, observed the same flag attached to Goguen's rear end.

The next day, the first police officer registered a complaint, claiming that Goguen had violated Massachusetts' flag misuse law. According to this law, "Whoever publicly mutilates, tramples upon, defaces or treats contemptuously the flag of the United States…, whether such flag is public or private property…, shall be punished by a fine of not less than ten nor more than one hundred dollars or by imprisonment for not more than one year, or both." The case went to trial, and the jury agreed with the police officer – Goguen had treated contemptuously the flag of the United States. Goguen was sentenced to six months in jail.

Goguen appealed, and the case ended up before the United States Supreme Court. In a 6-3 decision, the Court ruled in favor of Goguen, arguing that the wording of the Massachusetts flag misuse law was too vague – "contemptuous treatment" could mean almost anything.

Spence v. Washington

On May 10, 1970, three police officers saw an American flag hanging upside down from the window of an apartment building in Seattle, Washington. Attached to each side of the flag, and covering about half of the flag's surface, was a peace symbol made of removable black tape. The officers entered the main door of the apartment building, where they were met by Harold Spence, a college student. Spence said, "I suppose you are here about the flag. I didn't know there was anything wrong with it. I will take it down." He let the three officers into his apartment, whereupon the officers confiscated the flag and arrested Spence. Spence was cooperative; he didn't resist the arrest.

Spence was tried for violating Washington's flag misuse law. The relevant part of the law stated that no one shall place "any word, figure, mark, picture, design, drawing or advertisement of any nature upon any flag … of the United States," or display such a flag. During the trial, Spence testified that he placed the peace symbols on the flag and hung the flag from his window as a way to protest the recent American invasion of Cambodia and the subsequent shooting of protesters at Kent State University: "I felt there had been so much killing and that this was not what America stood for. I felt that the flag stood for America and I wanted people to know that I thought America stood for peace." Spence added that he made the peace symbols out of removable tape so that he could later remove the peace symbols without damaging the flag. The jury found Spence guilty, and the court sentenced Spence to ten days in jail, suspended, and a $75 fine.

On appeal, the United States Supreme Court, in a 6-3 decision, found the Washington flag misuse law unconstitutional, as it violated Spence's First Amendment right to freedom of speech.

An Amendment to the Constitution?

In 1989, in *Texas v. Johnson* – a case concerning a man who, to protest the policies of President Ronald Reagan, burned an American flag during the Republican National Convention in Dallas – the U.S. Supreme Court ruled yet again that desecration of the American flag is protected by the First Amendment to the U.S. Constitution. In response to this decision, an outraged Congress passed the Flag Protection Act, a piece of legislation that allowed the punishment of anyone who "knowingly mutilates, defaces, physically defiles, burns, maintains on the floor or ground, or tramples upon any U.S. flag." The following year, in 1990, the Supreme Court fired back, ruling in *U.S. v. Eichman* that the Flag Protection Act was unconstitutional.

Eichman left Congress only one option, if it wanted to protect the American flag from desecration – to pass an Amendment to the U.S. Constitution. Amending the Constitution isn't easy. To do so, two thirds of the House of Representatives and two thirds of the Senate must vote in support of the Amendment, and three quarters of the states must ratify the Amendment. Beginning in the 1990s, Congress voted – repeatedly, year after year – on a Flag Desecration Amendment, the text of which read, "The Congress shall have power to prohibit the physical desecration of the flag of the United States." To date, however, the Amendment has never gotten past the Senate. The closest vote came in 2006, when, after passing in the House of Representatives, the Amendment was defeated in the Senate by one vote. One of the thirty-four Senators who voted against the Amendment that year was future President Barack Obama.

Those who support a Flag Desecration Amendment often argue that the American flag is a sacred symbol deserving special protection. One of the things it symbolizes is, as the Pledge of Allegiance states, "one Nation under God, indivisible." Thus, to permit desecration of the flag is to permit protesters to attempt to divide the nation, which can only be harmful to America. Small wonder, then, that so many Americans find desecration of the flag seriously offensive. Besides, a ban on desecration of the flag isn't really a restriction on anyone's right to freedom of expression, since protesters can always find other ways to express dissatisfaction with their country. For example, instead of burning his flag, Sydney Street could have written a letter to the editor of a newspaper condemning the shooting of James Meredith. Similarly, instead of covering each side of his flag with a peace symbol, Harold Spence could have handed out leaflets condemning the invasion of Cambodia and the shootings at Kent State University.

Those who oppose a Flag Desecration Amendment often reply to these arguments that the American flag not only symbolizes "one Nation under God, indivisible," but also – as the Pledge of Allegiance likewise affirms – "liberty and justice for all." One of the liberties for which America stands is freedom of expression, a liberty embodied in the First Amendment. How ironic it would be to pass a Flag Desecration Amendment, restricting freedom of expression, when freedom of expression is one of the things the flag represents! The free exchange of ideas, even of ideas many Americans find seriously offensive, isn't harmful to America, but on the contrary is highly beneficial. It's only through the free exchange of ideas that we can hope to continue our progress toward the truth. Even ideas we feel certain are false, or repugnant, may for all we know turn out to be true. To suppose otherwise is to assume that we're infallible – and, as even a casual observation reveals, no one's infallible. Furthermore, just as allowing people to express their ideas is essential, so is allowing people to express those ideas in whatever manner they think most fitting. We may feel certain that desecrating the flag is an inappropriate manner of expressing dissatisfaction with our country, but we could be mistaken about this as well. To suppose otherwise is once again to assume that we're infallible.

Questions for reflection: How far should people's right to freedom of expression extend? Did Sydney Street, Stephen Radich, Valarie Goguen, or Harold Spence do anything wrong? Would a Flag Desecration Amendment be a good thing, or a bad thing?

Puzzle 14
Academic Freedom

October 28, 2014

    Cheryl Abbate, a Philosophy graduate student at Marquette University, a Catholic school in Milwaukee, Wisconsin, guides a discussion in "Theory of Ethics," the undergraduate course she teaches. The discussion is about John Rawls' Equal Liberty Principle, according to which each person has a right to the most extensive set of liberties that is compatible with an equal liberty for all. The goal of the discussion is to help students apply Rawls' principle to current issues. Students raise a number of current issues, including gun control, legalization of marijuana, and seat belt laws. Some issues are discussed at length; others are passed over quickly. One student suggests that Rawls' principle would allow gay marriage. Abbate agrees with the student, but doesn't elaborate, instead telling the class that, if anyone holds a different view, he or she should speak to her after class.

    When the class is over, a student who opposes gay marriage approaches Abbate. Without her knowledge, he records their conversation with his cell phone. The conversation proceeds as follows:

Student: I'm ... I have to say, I'm very disappointed in you.

Abbate: Okay, for what reason?

Student: We were talking today and you were kind of ... when we were talking today about gay marriage, you said "well obviously this one's [inaudible]." I have to be completely honest with you, I don't agree with gay marriage. There have been studies that show that children that are brought up in gay households do a lot worse in life such as test scores, in school, and in the real world. So, when you completely dismiss an entire argument based off of your personal views, it sets a precedent for the classroom that "oh my God, this is so wrong; you can't agree with this, you're a horrible person if you agree with this." And that's what came off. And I have to say I am very personally offended by that.

Abbate: Okay.

Student: And I would stress for you in your professional career going forward, you're going to be teaching for many more years, that you watch how you approach those issues because when you set a precedent like that, because you are the authority figure in the classroom, people truly do listen to you.

Abbate: Okay, I'm going to stop you right there. The question was about gay marriage. So, if you're going to bring statistics up about ... you know, single people can adopt children, right; you don't have to be married.

Student: Yes.

Abbate: So gay marriage has nothing to do with the adoption of children.

Student: I know, and one of the reasons why I'm against gay marriage is because that gay couples are allowed to adopt.

Abbate: Okay. Do you realize as an individual you can adopt a child on your own and then have a relationship with someone?

Student: Yes, absolutely.

Abbate: Even if it's not legal.

Student: Absolutely, and I'm not in agreement with that.

Abbate: I don't think gay marriage has ... first of all, I would really question those statistics.

Student: I'll send them to you.

Abbate: Just like you were going to send me the other statistics about tail docking and ...

Student: Tail docking?

Abbate: That it doesn't cause pain.

Student: Oh yeah, I'll send those to you as well.

Abbate: So, any research that you're going to have I'm really going to question it because there is a significant amount of pure research that says otherwise, but even setting that aside, the question is about gay marriage itself. It's not about adoption of children ...

Student: Absolutely, but there are different reasons why you can disagree with gay marriage.

Abbate: Okay.

Student: So.

Abbate: So, gay marriage isn't banned ... granting people license to have children, it has nothing to do with that? Do people have a right to marry someone of the same sex ...

Student: Regardless of why I'm against gay marriage, it's still wrong for the teacher of a class to completely discredit one person's opinion when they may have different opinions.

Abbate: Okay, there are some opinions that are not appropriate, that are harmful, such as racist opinions, sexist opinions, and quite honestly, do you know if anyone in the class is homosexual?

Student: No, I don't.

Abbate: And don't you think that that would be offensive to them if you were to raise your hand and challenge this?

Student: If I choose to challenge this, it's my right as an American citizen.

Abbate: Okay, well, actually you don't have a right in this class, as ... especially as an ethics professor to make homophobic comments, racist comments, sexist comments ...

Student: Homophobic comments? They're not. I'm not saying that gays, that one guy can't like another girl or something like that. Or one guy can't like another guy.

Abbate: This is about restricting rights and liberties of individuals. Um, and just as I would take offense if women can't serve in XYZ positions because that is a sexist comment.

Student: I don't have any problem with women saying that. I don't have any problem with women joining anything like that.

Abbate: No, I'm saying that if you are going to make a comment like that, it would be similar to making a ...

Student: Absolutely.

Abbate: How I would experience would be similar to how someone who is in this room and who is homosexual who would experience someone criticizing this.

Student: Okay, so because they are homosexual, I can't have my opinions? And it's not being offensive towards them because I am just having my opinions on a very broad subject.

Abbate: You can have whatever opinions you want, but I can tell you right now, in this class homophobic comments, racist comments, and sexist comments will not be tolerated. If you don't like that, you are more than free to drop this class.

Student: So, are you saying that not agreeing with gay marriage is homophobic?

Abbate: To argue about that individuals should not have rights is going to be offensive to someone in this class.

Student: I'm not saying rights, I'm saying one single right. Okay? So is that what you're saying? Are you saying that if I don't agree with gays being allowed to get married, that I am homophobic?

Abbate: I'm saying that it would come off as a homophobic comment in this class.

Student: That's not what you said two minutes ago. Two seconds ago, you just said that is a homophobic comment to disagree with gay marriage.

Abbate: No, the example that I gave was in this class, if you were going to make a comment about the restriction of the rights of women, such as saying that women can't serve ... Are you videotaping or taping this conversation?

Student: No.

Abbate: Can I see your phone?

Student: Oh, I am. I'm going to be showing it to your superiors.

Abbate: Okay, go ahead.
Student: Absolutely.

When the conversation ends, Abbate informs Sebastian Luft, Assistant Chair of the Philosophy Department, of the details of the incident. For his part, the student speaks with Susanne Foster, Associate Dean of the College of Arts & Sciences, who, in accordance with College policy, directs him to Nancy Snow, Chair of the Philosophy Department. The student meets with Snow the same day and, after weighing his options, decides to remain in Abbate's course. Later, however, he reverses his decision and drops the course.

November 9, 2014

John McAdams, a 69-year-old tenured Professor of Political Science known for his political conservatism, sends an email to Abbate telling her that he's working on a story about the confrontation she had with the student and that he would like her view of what happened. He knows about the incident because the student spoke to him about it, and shared with him the recording of the conversation he had on his cell phone. Several hours later, not having gotten a response from Abbate, McAdams proceeds to publish the following on his blog *The Marquette Warrior*:

A student we know was in a philosophy class ("Theory of Ethics"), and the instructor (one Cheryl Abbate) was attempting to apply a philosophical text to modern political controversies. So far so good.

She listed some issues on the board, and came to "gay rights." She then airily said that "everybody agrees on this, and there is no need to discuss it."

The student, a conservative who disagrees with some of the gay lobby's notions of "gay rights" (such as gay marriage), approached her after class and told her he thought the issue deserved to be discussed. Indeed, he told Abbate that if she dismisses an entire argument because of her personal views, that sets a terrible precedent for the class.

The student argued against gay marriage and gay adoption, and for a while Abbate made some plausible arguments to the student – pointing out that single people can adopt a child, so why not a gay couple? She even asked the student for research showing that children of gay parents do worse than children of straight, married parents. The student said he would provide it.

So far, this is the sort of argument that ought to happen in academia.

But then things deteriorated.

Abbate explained that "some opinions are not appropriate, such as racist opinions, sexist opinions" and then went on to ask, "Do you know if anyone in your class is homosexual?" And further, "don't you think it would be offensive to them" if some student raised his hand and challenged gay marriage? The point being, apparently, that any gay classmates should not be subjected to hearing any disagreement with their presumed policy views.

Then things deteriorated further as the student said that it was his right as an American citizen to make arguments against gay marriage. Abbate replied that "you don't have a right in this class to make homophobic comments."

She further said she would "take offense" if the student said that women can't serve in particular roles. And she added that somebody who is homosexual would experience similar offense if somebody opposed gay marriage in class.

She went on, "In this class, homophobic comments, racist comments, will not be tolerated." She then invited the student to drop the class.

Which the student is doing.

Abbate, of course, was just using a tactic typical among liberals now. Opinions with which they disagree are not merely wrong, and are not to be argued against on their merits, but are deemed "offensive" and need to be shut up.

As Charles Krauthammer explained:

The proper word for that attitude is totalitarian. It declares certain controversies over and visits serious consequences – from social ostracism to vocational defenestration – upon those who refuse to be silenced.

The newest closing of the leftist mind is on gay marriage. Just as the science of global warming is settled, so, it seems, are the moral and philosophical merits of gay marriage.

To oppose it is nothing but bigotry, akin to racism. Opponents are to be similarly marginalized and shunned, destroyed personally and professionally.

Of course, only certain groups have the privilege of shutting up debate. Things thought to be "offensive" to gays, blacks, women, and so on must be stifled. Further, it's not considered necessary to actually find out what the group really thinks. "Women" are supposed to feel warred upon when somebody opposes abortion, but in the real world men and women are equally likely to oppose abortion.

The same is true of Obama's contraception mandate.

But in the politically correct world of academia, one is supposed to assume that all victim groups think the same way as leftist professors.

Groups not favored by leftist professors, of course, can be freely attacked, and their views (or supposed views) ridiculed. Christians and Muslims are not allowed to be "offended" by pro-gay comments.

(Muslims are a protected victim group in lots of other ways, but not this one.)

And it is a free fire zone where straight white males are concerned.

The student first complained to the office of the Dean of Arts & Sciences, and talked to an Associate Dean, one Susanne Foster. Foster sent the student to the Chair of the Philosophy Department, saying that department chairs usually handle such cases. The chair, Nancy Snow, pretty much blew off the issue.

Interestingly, both Snow and Foster have been involved in cases of politically correct attacks on free expression at Marquette.

Foster took offense when one of her colleagues referred to a dinner which happened to involve only female faculty as a "girls' night out." He was reprimanded by then department chair James South for "sexism," but the reprimand was overturned by Marquette.

Snow, in a class on the "Philosophy of Crime and Punishment" tried to shut up a student who offered a response, from the perspective of police, to Snow's comments about supposed "racial profiling." The student said talk about racial profiling makes life hard for cops, since it may make minorities hostile and uncooperative.

Snow tried to silence him, claiming "this is a diverse class." This was an apparent reference to two black students in the class, who were, Snow assumed, likely offended on hearing that.

The majority of the class, contacted by The Marquette Warrior, felt the comments were reasonable and relevant, but Snow insisted that the student write an apology to the black students.

So how is a student to get vindication from University officials who hold the same intolerant views as Abbate?

Thus the student is dropping the class, and will have to take another Philosophy class in the future.

But this student is rather outspoken and assertive about his beliefs. That puts him among a small minority of Marquette students. How many students, especially in politically correct departments like Philosophy, simply stifle their disagreement, or worse yet get indoctrinated into the views of the instructor, since those are the only ideas allowed, and no alternative views are aired?

Like the rest of academia, Marquette is less and less a real university. And when gay marriage cannot be discussed, certainly not a Catholic university.

January 30, 2015

In a 15-page letter to McAdams, Richard Holz, Dean of the College of Arts & Sciences, explains why Marquette University is revoking McAdams' tenure and dismissing him from the faculty. Revoking tenure is a serious matter, undertaken only in extreme circumstances. According to Marquette's Faculty Statutes, the circumstances warranting revocation of tenure "arise from a faculty member's conduct which clearly and substantially fails to meet the standards of personal and professional excellence which generally characterizes University faculties, but only if through this conduct a faculty member's value will probably be substantially impaired." The conduct that leads to the revocation of McAdams' tenure and his dismissal centers on his November 9 blog about the confrontation between Abbate and the student. Holz raises a number of concerns:

1. McAdams' blog made several false and misleading claims: *[Y]ou gave an account of what happened in a class you did not attend and was not taped, describing Ms. Abbate as "airily" making a statement about "gay rights...." Likewise, when you criticized the Department Chair for not taking action, you once again either were recklessly unaware that the student did not give Dr. Snow the same information he gave you – namely a tape of the conversation – or again you elected not to include these facts in your Internet story. Further, in asserting that the Department Chair "pretty much blew off the issue," you either were recklessly unaware of, or you ignored, the fact that two days after meeting with the Chair, the student wrote to thank her and the Assistant Chair for their time and attention to his concerns.... Moreover, you stated in your Internet story only that the College of Arts & Sciences "sent" the student to the Department with his complaint. Once again you either were recklessly unaware of, or you ignored, the fact that the student was expressly told he could come back to the College if he was "dissatisfied" with how the Department handled his concerns.... [Y]ou implied that as a result of the exchange you had recounted the student had dropped the class.... That is false. As you knew or should have known, the student told the University three days after withdrawing that he had done so because he was getting an "F" at midterm. He further specifically agreed that his grade fairly reflected his performance and had nothing to do with his political or personal beliefs.... To endure, a scholar-teacher's academic freedom must be grounded on competence and integrity, including accuracy "at all times," a respect for others' opinions, and the exercise of appropriate restraint. Without adherence to these standards, those such as yourself invested with tenure's power can carelessly and arrogantly intimidate and silence the less-powerful and then raise the shields of academic freedom and free expression against all attempts to stop such abuse.*

2. McAdams used Abbate's name in his blog without first securing her permission, despite past warnings not to use students' names: *In March 2008, you published the name of a student who worked in advertising for the* MARQUETTE TRIBUNE *after she had declined to run an advertisement highlighting alleged risks from the "morning after" pill. Only after that student contacted you to advise of the impacts upon her and to request you to cease and desist did you delete her name. In March 2011, you published blog posts regarding a student who was helping to organize a campus performance of* THE VAGINA

MONOLOGUES. *Again, the harmful consequences of your unilateral naming of students were pointed out. You acknowledged at that time that publishing student names on the Internet was a matter of concern, but given your naming of Ms. Abbate that acknowledgment from 2011 appears to be without meaning or effect.*

3. Because McAdams used her name, Abbate received threatening hate mail and feared for her safety: *As a result of your unilateral, dishonorable, and irresponsible decision to publicize the name of our graduate student, and your decision to publish information that was false and materially misleading about her and your University colleagues, that student received a series of hate-filled and despicable emails, including one suggesting that she had committed "treason and sedition" and as a result faced penalties such as "drawing, hanging, beheading, and quartering." Another note, delivered to her campus mailbox, told the student, "You must undo the terrible wrong committed when you were born. Your mother failed to make the right choice. You must abort yourself for the glory of inclusiveness and tolerance." Accordingly, and understandably, the student feared for her personal safety, and we posted a Public Safety Officer outside her classroom. In addition, as a result of your conduct and its consequences, Ms. Cheryl Abbate now has withdrawn from our graduate program and moved to another University to continue her academic career.*

4. McAdams' blog intimidates other instructors and students: *[Y]our conduct creates fear in your colleagues and students that their actions and words will, at your unilateral "discretion," be put on the Internet in a distorted fashion. Consequently, faculty members have voiced concerns about how they could become targets in your blog based upon items they might choose to include in a class syllabus. Your conduct thus impairs the very freedoms of teaching and expression that you vehemently purport to promote.*

February 4, 2015

McAdams responds to Dean Holz's letter, stating that he has "excellent legal counsel, and most certainly will not go quietly."

2019

McAdams indeed did not go quietly. The case made its way to the Wisconsin Supreme Court, which ruled, by a four to two margin, in favor of McAdams, requiring Marquette to reinstate him with back pay. As for Abbate, she recently completed her Ph.D. in Philosophy at the University of Colorado. Her dissertation was about animal rights.

Questions for reflection: Did Abbate's student have a right to express his opinion about gay marriage in her class? Should racist, sexist, or homophobic opinions not be allowed in a college classroom? Did McAdams say anything inappropriate in his blog of November 9? Did Marquette University do the right thing by revoking McAdams' tenure and dismissing him from its faculty?

Puzzle 15
Legalization of Drugs

For as long as Stuart could remember, the recreational use of drugs – marijuana, heroin, cocaine, and others – had been illegal. Today, however, that could change, depending on the vote that parliament was about to take. Stuart already knew how most members of parliament would vote. About half favored legalization of drugs, while the other half opposed. Only two or three were still undecided. Stuart was one of those two or three. His vote, he knew, could prove to be the deciding vote – that was how evenly divided parliament was.

To help him make up his mind, he reflected on past votes he had cast as a member of parliament. There was, for example, that curious vote a couple of years back about voluntary slavery. Slavery, of course, had been abolished long ago, well before Stuart had gotten involved in politics. When it was abolished, the law presumed that the slave was an unwilling victim – a seemingly safe presumption, for why would anyone *willingly* become a slave? Yet a couple of years ago, a small but growing number of citizens, who had formed the Freedom under Slavery Society, or FUSS, argued that, in a liberal nation that espouses the right to liberty, a person should be free to become the slave, once and for all, of a willing master. Several members of FUSS even carried through with their beliefs, signing contracts that placed them forever under slavery. Some of these slaves seemed content with their lot, while others came to regret their choice. But even this latter group acknowledged that a contract was a contract and that they knew what they were getting themselves into when they signed on the dotted line. FUSS had become sufficiently influential that parliament felt a need to take action.

For his part, Stuart agreed with FUSS that the right to liberty should extend as widely as possible. Yet he also understood that people shouldn't be free to do just anything. No one, for example, has a right to murder, rape, or rob – such a right, though granting freedom to the perpetrator, would interfere with the freedom of the victim. After giving the matter due thought, Stuart concluded that becoming a slave was one of the things people shouldn't be free to do. Voluntary slavery, after all, was tantamount to the freedom to give up, once and for all, all of one's freedoms. Such a freedom – like the freedom to murder, rape, or rob – didn't maximize liberty, but on the contrary infringed on liberty, and hence was incompatible with the right to liberty. In an impassioned speech to his fellow members of parliament, Stuart advanced this argument, which carried the day. Voluntary slavery, like involuntary slavery, became illegal.

As Stuart recalled his argument against involuntary slavery, it occurred to him that a similar argument might be advanced against the legalization of drugs. The first time one uses a drug, one makes a free choice. But drugs – especially the more potent ones, such as cocaine – are addictive. Soon enough the user becomes, in effect, a slave to the dug. Drug use is thus similar to voluntary slavery – both amount to the freedom to give up all of one's freedoms. If the one is wrong, so must be the other. If the one should be illegal, so should the other. Perhaps, Stuart thought to himself, he should vote against the legalization of drugs – especially the more potent drugs.

But then he remembered another vote he had cast as a member of parliament. Shortly after he became a lawmaker nearly three years ago, the Society against Drunkenness, or SAD, had lobbied parliament to introduce a bill that would make the manufacture, sale, and consumption of alcohol illegal. Stuart had had serious reservations about the bill – the U.S. experiment with Prohibition, after all, had been an unmitigated disaster, and Stuart couldn't think of any reason it would work better in his own country. The bill, however, did force him to think hard about exactly what the right to liberty entailed.

Initially, he thought that what made acts such as murder, rape, and robbery wrong was that they harmed others. Perhaps, then, the right to liberty involved the harm principle – that people should be free to do anything, except harm others. Most of Stuart's fellow lawmakers disagreed with the harm principle. They believed that the role of government included preventing people not only from harming others but also from harming themselves. Thus, a little while back, parliament passed a law requiring drivers and their passengers to wear seatbelts. It passed this law not because the refusal to wear a seatbelt would harm others, but because, if one got into an accident, one would more likely harm oneself. Stuart agreed that wearing a seatbelt was prudent – when he was in a car, he always wore one himself. But he didn't think government should prevent people from harming themselves. It seemed to him that governing officials had no special expertise in what counts as a harm, that the person most likely to know what harms an individual is that individual. Hence, individuals should decide for themselves what's harmful to them, such as whether or not to wear a seatbelt – or smoke cigarettes or gamble away their life savings.

The same, Stuart thought, was true of drinking alcohol. Excessive drinking might harm oneself – by damaging one's liver, staining one's reputation, or interfering with clear thinking. But people should be free to harm themselves. Of course, excessive drinking causes some people to become violent. In a drunken rage, these people may harm others. But even here, it seemed to Stuart, the crime wasn't the drinking but the act of violence. The act of violence should be illegal, but not the drinking.

All of this seemed to make sense – until Stuart found a fatal flaw in the harm principle. According to the harm principle, we may harm ourselves but not others. But isn't it true that whenever we harm ourselves, we inevitably also harm others? If, for example, Stuart were to drink himself to death, wouldn't he harm not just himself but also his wife and friends, because they depended on him and enjoyed his company? Clearly, Stuart needed a different principle.

After some further thought, he formulated the obligations principle – that people should be free to do anything, except violate distinct and assignable obligations to others. Stuart didn't bother to define "distinct and assignable obligations," but he thought the term was sufficiently clear to determine whether drinking alcohol should be legal. Suppose, for instance, that a police officer gets drunk while on duty. This, Stuart thought, should be illegal, because the police officer has a distinct and assignable obligation to protect the community and getting drunk interferes with his ability to carry out that obligation. Suppose, however, that the police officer gets drunk while off duty. Because he's off duty, he's relieved of his distinct and assignable obligation to protect the community. In Stuart's view, the police officer, under these circumstances, should be allowed by law to get drunk – at least as long as he sobers up by the time he returns to duty. Armed with the obligations principle, Stuart voted against the SAD bill.

The application of the obligations principle to the legalization of drugs seemed straightforward. Indeed, Stuart thought, wasn't alcohol itself a drug, even more potent than some of the things people called drugs? If Stuart agreed that drinking alcohol should be legal, shouldn't he similarly agree that using drugs should be legal – as long as, in using drugs, one doesn't violate any distinct and assignable obligations to others? Just as the police officer shouldn't get drunk while on duty, so he shouldn't smoke marijuana or snort cocaine. But if he's not on duty, he should be allowed to drink or use drugs.

So Stuart felt conflicted. On the one hand, the obligations principle seemed to imply that the recreational use of drugs should be legal. But on the other hand, insofar as the recreational use of drugs resembled voluntary slavery, it seemed that it should be illegal. Stuart wasn't sure which argument was stronger. Yet he couldn't mull on it any further, because it was time for him to cast his vote.

Questions for reflection: Should the recreational use of drugs be legalized? Does it matter what the drug is – for example, should the recreational use of marijuana, but not heroin or cocaine, be legalized? Is the recreational use of drugs analogous to voluntary slavery? Is it analogous to drinking alcohol? Should we adopt the harm principle? Should we adopt the obligations principle?

Puzzle 16
Extreme Poverty

Imagine making less than US$1.25 a day, an amount that the World Bank identifies as marking extreme poverty. Imagine trying, on that income, to provide for yourself and your family. How would you get enough food to fend off malnutrition and starvation? Would you be able to access clean drinking water? What would you do for shelter – would your family be homeless? How would you clothe and educate your children? And what if you got sick? You wouldn't be able to afford quality health care, and if your illness persisted or worsened you might not be able to work. If this happened, you and your family would face even bigger problems than you already had.

These are the circumstances of a billion people, about 15% of the world's population. The large majority of these people – 85% of them – live in just twenty countries, most of them in South Asia, Southeast Asia, and Sub-Saharan Africa. The US$1.25 a day that defines extreme poverty is not what US$1.25 could buy in these twenty countries, which might be significantly more than what US$1.25 could buy in the United States. Instead, what people in extreme poverty live on each day, in their own currency, is less than the purchasing power that US$1.25 has in the United States. This isn't just poverty. As Robert McNamara, who served thirteen years as President of the World Bank, once put it, it's "life at the very margin of existence ... a condition of life so characterized by malnutrition, illiteracy, disease, squalid surroundings, high infant mortality, and low life expectancy as to be beneath any reasonable definition of human decency."

The United States has its poor, but poverty in the U.S. isn't nearly as extreme as poverty in those twenty countries containing 85% of the world's extremely poor. The U.S. Census Bureau sets the poverty line in the U.S. at an annual income of $12,490 for an individual and $25,750 for a family of four. This comes to more than $34 a day for an individual and more than $70 a day for a family of four – far more than $1.25 a day. About three quarters of Americans in poverty own a car, about three quarters have air conditioning, and 97% own a color TV. Poor Americans can send their children to school for free through high school, and Medicaid helps give them access to health care. For those who have a medical emergency and cannot afford treatment, the cost of their treatment is borne by taxpayers. No doubt, America's poor suffer hardships, and in a country as affluent as the United States this is a disgrace. Just as clearly, though, America's poor suffer much, much less than do the extremely poor in other countries.

Extreme poverty kills. Whereas life expectancy in wealthy nations is approximately seventy-eight years, in the least developed countries it is less than fifty years. Whereas in wealthy nations not even one in a hundred children dies before the age of five, in the poorest parts of the world one in five dies. Almost ten million younger children, and another eight million older children and adults, die each year from causes related to poverty. Some of these people die from malnutrition, others from diseases such as malaria, measles, or diarrhea. They often get diseases because they don't have access to clean drinking water, and they often die from them because they don't have access to adequate health care. In wealthy countries, the diseases that kill people in poor countries either don't exist or are rarely fatal.

Contrasting with the billion people living in extreme poverty are the billion people living in affluence. These billion people can provide themselves with adequate food, water, shelter, clothing, sanitation, education, and health care – and after satisfying these needs they still have money they can use for other purposes. Many of the world's affluent spend much or all of their spare cash on luxuries for themselves – a vacation in the Swiss alps, a sporty BMW, a $5,000 Rolex, all seventy-nine episodes of the original Star Trek series. Some spend truly vast sums for just a single luxury. For example, in 2003 Paul Allen, who became a billionaire after starting a computer company called Microsoft with Bill Gates, purchased a $200 million 413-foot yacht called *Octopus*, at the time the world's largest. In 2005 the cofounders of Google, Larry Page and Sergey Brin, bought a Boeing 767 and modified it for their private use. The jet's estimated value: $25 million. In 2006 Anousheh Ansari, an Iranian-American engineer, paid $20 million for the rare privilege of taking a flight to the International Space Station that orbits the earth. When asked why she wanted to do this, she answered, "I hope to inspire everyone – especially young people, women, and young girls all over the world, and in Middle Eastern countries that do not provide women with the same opportunities as men – to not give up their dreams and to pursue them."

In light of all the extreme poverty in the world, the question arises whether anything is wrong with such profligate spending. Do those who spend $1,000 on Star Trek episodes or $200 million on a yacht undervalue the vital interests of the poor? Would donating $20 million to the cause of overcoming extreme poverty do more "to inspire everyone" than taking a $20 million space flight? Should the affluent forgo some of their luxuries? Should they do more to help the desperately poor? Many arguments in defense of spending on luxuries rather than on the poor are possible. One of these arguments appeals to the right to liberty – the liberty to dispose of one's wealth as one sees fit.

Many wealthy people – the argument goes – work hard for their money. They may spend years acquiring the necessary education, and more years working their way up the corporate ladder. Along the way, they may make sacrifices – sixty- or seventy-hour work weeks, exhausting business trips, time spent away from family. Those who make money through their own effort like this should be free to do with that money as they like. After all, it's their hard-won money, not anyone else's. If they want to give it away to the desperately poor, they certainly may. But if they prefer to spend it on luxuries for themselves or their family, they do nothing wrong. The only money the poor are entitled to is the money they earn with the sweat of their own brows, and the only right they have against the wealthy is that the wealthy not harm them. The wealthy may not kill them or rape them or enslave them, but the wealthy are under no obligation to help them. Any redistribution of wealth from the rich to the poor that the rich don't voluntarily undertake is a form of theft, and theft of any kind shouldn't be tolerated.

Is this argument convincing? Does it exculpate those who turn a blind eye to the suffering of the poor? Some philosophers have doubts. In the first place, even if the wealthy have a right to spend their money on luxuries for themselves rather than using it to help the poor, it doesn't follow that, if this is what they do, they do nothing wrong. Sometimes people ought to share, even if they have a right not to. For instance, suppose a child is given a box of chocolates for her birthday. Her face lights up as she opens the present – chocolates are among her favorite things to eat. And eat them she does, one after another after another, even as her little brother looks on with envy. He asks his sister if she'd please share some of the chocolates with him, but she refuses, tightening her grip on the box as she continues to eat. She may have a right to eat all the chocolates, since they were a gift to her alone, not to her and her brother jointly. Yet refusing to share seems wrong – it's selfish. Similarly, one might argue that the affluent are selfish when they buy a $5,000 Rolex instead of a $30 but quite accurate Timex, leaving $4,970 with which they could have helped the poor.

All of this grants that the wealthy at least have a right not to share. According to some philosophers, however, this is granting too much. To a considerable extent, how much wealth one has depends on luck – for example, whether one is born into a wealthy or a poor family, whether one's parents do or don't support their children's education, and whether one's society values or doesn't value the talents one happens to have. Thus, LeBron James is wealthy not just because he's a talented and hard-working basketball player, but because American society happens to value basketball. Had he been born and raised in a different society, one that cares little or nothing about basketball, his life prospects might have been very different. But even James' talent for basketball and his work ethic may largely be a result of luck, depending on the genes he inherited from his parents and the way his parents raised him, neither of which he had any control over. If, however, the wealth one has depends so much on luck, it's no longer clear that one is entitled to this wealth. Imagine you're about to be born into either an affluent family in the United States or an extremely poor family in Malawi, but you don't know which. Would you support an ethic that gives Americans a right not to share, or would you support some redistribution of wealth from the United States to Malawi? Redistribution of wealth from the lucky to the unlucky may be morally required.

Finally, one might argue that affluent people often acquire or use their wealth in ways that harm the poor. They may pollute the atmosphere, overfish the oceans, or deforest the land, all of which can deprive poor people of their meager livelihood. Or they may purchase products that are cheaply made in the sweatshops of developing countries, or products that contribute to global warming, the effects of which hit the poor harder than the wealthy. Consider the sporty BMW you buy, as opposed to something more fuel-efficient. Or consider Paul Allen's $200 million yacht, Larry Page and Sergey Brin's $25 million Boeing 767, or Anousheh Ansari's $20 million space flight. The result of all these purchases is a significant increase in greenhouse gas emissions, which, by contributing to global warming, disproportionately harms the poor. Surely, therefore, it's a mistake to say that the affluent have a right to do with their money whatever they like. Surely it's morally better to help the poor than to harm them.

Questions for reflection: Should the affluent do more to help the desperately poor? Do the desperately poor have a right to receive help from the affluent, or do they have only a right not to be harmed? What is the best way to solve the problem of extreme poverty?

PART III
Who Has Rights

Puzzle 17
Roe v. Wade

The Plaintiff

Norma McCorvey had a tough childhood. Her father left the family when she was thirteen, and her mother was a violent alcoholic. At age fourteen, after having been raped at a reform school, McCorvey dropped out of school. Two years later, she got married, but then separated from her husband when he started beating her. By the time she was twenty-one, she had already given birth to two children, each having a different father, and she was pregnant with a third child.

The first child was raised by McCorvey's mother, the second by the child's father. McCorvey didn't want to have a third child; she wanted to get an abortion. But it was 1969, and she was living in Texas. At that time, abortion was illegal in Texas, except in cases of rape or incest, or when a woman needed an abortion to save her life. McCorvey claimed – falsely – that she had been raped, but her scheme fell apart when she was unable to produce evidence of rape. She considered traveling to California, where the law was less restrictive, and getting an abortion there, but she didn't have enough money for that. Finally, she attempted to visit an illegal abortion clinic in Dallas, but that didn't work either, because authorities had already shut the clinic down. McCorvey appeared to be out of options.

That was when two lawyers – Linda Coffee and Sarah Weddington – approached her. Coffee and Weddington hoped to file a class-action lawsuit that would challenge the constitutionality of the Texas abortion law. To file the lawsuit, they needed a plaintiff. They asked McCorvey if she'd be willing to be the plaintiff. The only condition was that McCorvey not get an abortion before the case was decided – if she did, the court might rule that the case was moot and thus do nothing to change the law. McCorvey agreed to the terms.

Unfortunately for McCorvey, the case dragged on – she gave birth to a girl, which she gave up for adoption. Eventually, in December 1971, when the girl was two years old, the case came before the United States Supreme Court. The case was *Roe v. Wade*. McCorvey, assigned the name Jane Roe to protect her privacy, found herself involved in what would be one of the most famous court cases of all time.

The Decision

The Supreme Court handed down its landmark 7-2 decision on January 23, 1973. Ruling against the Texas law, the majority of the justices declared that women have a constitutional right to get an abortion. Before *Roe*, it was up to each state whether or not to allow abortions. Some states did, but most, like Texas, didn't – except in extreme circumstances such as rape. After *Roe*, however, all states had to allow abortions – though states could still place certain restrictions on abortion.

To reach its decision, the Court addressed three questions:

1) Does a woman seeking an abortion have a right to privacy? A right to privacy is a right to do something without interference from the state. In the United States people's right to privacy is extensive, but it's also limited. Thus, I may get drunk, but I may not drink and drive. I may smoke, but I may not puff smoke in other people's faces. I may view pornographic materials, but I may not view child pornography. What, then, about a woman who wishes to terminate her pregnancy? Should she be allowed to do so without interference from the state? The Supreme Court admitted that, just as the state has a legitimate interest in protecting people from drunk drivers and secondhand smoke and pedophiles, so it has a legitimate interest in protecting fetuses. It has this interest because fetuses represent the future of society and the state has a legitimate interest in the future of society. But does the state's interest in protecting fetuses carry greater weight than a woman's desire to terminate her pregnancy, or does a woman's desire to terminate her pregnancy carry greater weight than the state's interest in protecting fetuses? According to the Court, the answer depends on whether the fetus is viable. A fetus is said to be viable if it can be removed from the womb and still survive, either with or without the aid of machinery, such as respirators. The Court determined, then, that a woman seeking an abortion has a right to privacy, but only before her fetus is viable. Once the fetus becomes viable, the state's interest in protecting the fetus takes precedence. (In 1973 a fetus became viable around twenty-six weeks after conception, or at the beginning of the third trimester of pregnancy. Today, thanks to improved technology, the point at which fetuses become viable occurs earlier in pregnancy – some fetuses are viable as early as twenty

weeks after conception, and most are viable twenty-four weeks after conception.)

2) Is abortion a medically safe procedure for the woman? To answer the second question, the justices of the Supreme Court turned to the considered judgments of physicians. Physicians reported that, during the first trimester of pregnancy, abortion is reasonably safe, but is only sometimes safe thereafter. The Court accepted this view. (Today abortion is somewhat safer than it was in 1973: less than 1% of women who have abortions experience major complications, and the probability of a woman dying from an abortion is eleven times lower than the probability of a woman dying from childbirth, although the exact risk of death associated with abortion increases as the pregnancy continues. If an abortion is performed within the first eight weeks of pregnancy, the risk of death is one in a million; if it is performed more than twenty weeks after conception, the risk of death is one in 11,000.)

3) Is a fetus a person? According to the Court, this question is the most important of the three. For suppose it turns out that a fetus is a person. Since the Constitution accords all persons a right to life, a fetus would have a right to life, and, since an abortion would kill the fetus, an abortion would violate the fetus' right to life. Thus, if a fetus is a person, the Court would have had to rule against abortion rights – no matter how the Court answered the first two questions. But is a fetus a person? The Court noted that the experts on this question – doctors, theologians, and philosophers – were divided. Some insisted that a fetus is a person, while others were equally convinced that a fetus isn't a person. Since the experts had yet to reach a consensus, the Court concluded that, at least for the time being, the answer to the third question is unknown. The Court therefore felt compelled to base its decision solely on the answers it gave to the first two questions. (The question whether a fetus is a person continues to be controversial in the twenty-first century. Doctors, theologians, and philosophers are no closer to reaching a consensus.)

The Court summed up its decision as follows. A woman has an absolute right to get an abortion during the first trimester of her pregnancy. After the first trimester but before the fetus is viable, the only grounds the state can have for preventing an abortion is if the attending physicians determine that an abortion would put the woman's life or health at risk. Once the fetus is viable, though, the state may refuse to allow an abortion.

McCorvey's Conversion

For a decade after *Roe v. Wade*, Norma McCorvey remained anonymous – and poor. Without even a high school education, she could get only low-paying jobs such as waitressing and bartending. In the 1980s she revealed to the public that she was Jane Roe. She received a flurry of attention and got a job at a women's clinic. In 1994, with the help of a coauthor, she wrote about her life in *I Am Roe*.

Then came an astonishing turn of events. Operation Rescue, an antiabortion organization, set up an office in Dallas, next to the women's clinic where McCorvey worked. McCorvey was initially unsympathetic to Operation Rescue's activities, but eventually, while taking cigarette breaks, she befriended Philip Benham, a preacher who worked with Operation Rescue. Benham persuaded her to attend church, and she soon converted to Roman Catholicism. On August 8, 1995, in a backyard pool in Dallas, she was baptized. Shortly after, she publicly announced that she was now opposed to abortion.

In 1998, with the help of another coauthor, McCorvey wrote a second book, *Won by Love*. In this book, she explained what led her to become an antiabortionist:

> I was sitting in O.R.'s [Operation Rescue's] offices when I noticed a fetal development poster. The progression was so obvious, the eyes were so sweet. It hurt my heart, just looking at them. I ran outside and finally, it dawned on me. "Norma," I said to myself, "they're right." I had worked with pregnant women for years. I had been through three pregnancies and deliveries myself. I should have known. Yet something in that poster made me lose my breath. I kept seeing the picture of that tiny, 10-week-old embryo, and I said to myself, that's a baby! It's as if blinders just fell off my eyes and I suddenly understood the truth – that's a baby!

In this passage, McCorvey claimed to know what the justices of the Supreme Court claimed not to know – that a fetus, even as young as ten weeks after conception, is a baby, a person. Was McCorvey right?

Questions for reflection: What is a person? Is a fetus a person? If a fetus is a person, does it follow that abortion is wrong? Did the Supreme Court reach the right decision in Roe v. Wade, *or was its decision a mistake?*

Puzzle 18
Gay Marriage

On Valentine's Day in 2003, a gay couple appeared on the local news. Recognizing the two men, I turned up the volume on my TV. They were my neighbors, living together across the breezeway from the apartment my wife and I rented. Sometimes, as my wife and I would take an evening stroll through the apartment complex, we'd pass by the couple, who were likewise enjoying an after-dinner walk. We'd say "Hello" to them, and they'd say "Hello" to us. One of them, sensing the love my wife and I shared as we clasped hands, would smile broadly at us. His smile was infectious – we couldn't help but smile back.

On that Valentine's Day the two men had joined a handful of supporters of gay rights – there couldn't have been more than eight or ten of them – and converged on the town hall to demand the right of gay couples to marry. A news reporter appeared on the scene, the story having been deemed worthy enough to merit ninety seconds of airtime on the six o'clock news. During the interview, my neighbors stated that they'd been a couple for twenty years, that they loved each other just as any man and woman loved each other, and that getting married would mean as much to them as it would to any heterosexual couple. They claimed that barring gay and lesbian marriages was unjustified discrimination. Although they spoke to the reporter calmly and respectfully, their eyes were lit with a fiery passion for their cause.

I sympathized with my neighbors, and wished them luck. But at the time not a single state in the U.S. recognized gay marriage. Only a tiny number of protesters had showed up at the town hall, and after the story aired everyone went back to his or her daily life, apparently forgetting about gay rights. It seemed that my neighbors' dream of getting married was destined to go unfulfilled – at least for the foreseeable future.

Little did I know then that momentous changes were just around the corner. In May 2004, a little over a year after I saw my neighbors on TV, Massachusetts became the first state to recognize same-sex marriage. Four years later Connecticut, the state in which I and the gay couple lived, joined Massachusetts. By the end of 2014 thirty-five states had legalized gay marriage and three more – Alabama, Kansas, and Missouri – recognized gay marriage with restrictions. Today all fifty states must allow same-sex marriage, thanks to the 2015 landmark Supreme Court ruling in *Obergefell v. Hodges*.

Intense controversy, however, remains. The Supreme Court decision was handed down by the barest of margins, with five justices concurring and four dissenting. After the decision several counties, mainly in Alabama, defiantly refused to issue marriage licenses to same-sex couples, and millions of Americans continue to be personally opposed to gay marriage, no matter what the Supreme Court says. All of this opposition has several sources.

1) The argument from scripture. A handful of passages in the Bible appear to condemn homosexuality. For example, Leviticus 18:22 states, "You shall not lie with a male as with a woman; it is an abomination." Leviticus 20:13 says the same thing, and then adds a punishment for those who commit this abomination: "They shall be put to death; their blood is upon them." Many people who oppose gay marriage cite passages such as these. Their argument is that gay marriage is wrong because scripture holds that it's wrong.

Supporters of gay marriage might object to this argument in either of two ways. First, they might claim that, even if scripture holds that gay marriage is wrong, it doesn't follow that gay marriage is in fact wrong, for the simple reason that scripture could be mistaken. That the Bible is sometimes mistaken should come as no surprise, given that the authors of the Bible lived many centuries ago, in a more benighted age. The Copernican revolution, calculus, quantum physics, democracy, human rights – these, and a great many more, developments were beyond the imaginative powers of anyone living in those times. 1 Kings 7:23 asserts that a circle with a diameter of ten cubits would have a circumference of thirty cubits. But this is inaccurate. In fact, the circumference would be 31.4159… cubits. The author of 1 Kings was inaccurate because he knew nothing about π. In 1 Timothy 2:12 Paul writes, "I permit no woman to teach or to have authority over men; she is to keep silent." But Paul lived in a sexist society, and seems to have internalized its sexism. We who live in the twenty-first century know better the intelligence and value that women have. We thus know that Paul was mistaken. Similarly, then, even if the Bible holds that gay marriage is wrong, nothing follows. Gay marriage could still be perfectly acceptable.

Second, supporters of gay marriage might claim that, in spite of appearances, the Bible doesn't condemn homosexuality. Take, for example, the two passages from Leviticus quoted above. According to some biblical scholars, these are not condemnations of homosexuality, but only of a particular form of homosexual behavior called pederasty. Pederasty refers to homosexual relations between an adult male and a male adolescent. Such relations may be objectionable because a male adolescent might not be capable of fully free and informed consent to engage in homosexual activity. The case is different, however, when it comes to two adult males or two adult females. Thus, the Bible may not imply that anything is wrong with gay marriage between consenting adults.

2) The argument from nature. In Romans 1:26-27 Paul appears to disapprove of gay and lesbian activity, doing so on the grounds that it's unnatural: "Their women exchanged natural intercourse for unnatural, and in the same way also the men, giving up natural intercourse with women, were consumed with passion for one another." The argument that homosexuality is wrong because it's unnatural is common. Many opponents of gay marriage advance this argument.

One problem facing this argument is that those who advance it rarely take the time to spell out what they mean by "natural" and "unnatural." Some seem to mean by "natural" little more than whatever they happen to like, and by "unnatural" little more than whatever they happen to dislike. But this way of defining "natural" and "unnatural" hardly makes for a persuasive case against gay marriage, since the question remains why one should dislike gay marriage. More careful definitions are in order.

Sometimes we use the word "natural" to mean what all, most, or many people do, believe, or approve. Thus, we might say that it's only natural to wonder what happens to us when we die, because a great many people wonder about this. But even if most people disapprove of gay marriage – which we won't know until we've conducted the appropriate polls – it doesn't follow that gay marriage is wrong, since the majority of people could be in error. At one time, for instance, most people believed that the earth is the center of the universe, that only human beings make and use tools, and that women should not be allowed to vote. There are now good reasons to think that these beliefs were mistaken. But if people could be mistaken about these things, how do we know they're not likewise mistaken in their opposition to gay marriage?

At other times we use the word "natural" to mean what is instinctive or what is in our genes or what is consistent with the way we evolved. This is the sense we have in mind when we say that it's natural for a baby to suck its thumb. Researchers have gathered a wealth of evidence suggesting that homosexuality has at least some genetic basis. To the extent that it does, it's natural in the sense we're considering. Some argue, however, that homosexuality is unnatural because it's inconsistent with the way we evolved – same-sex relations don't help homosexuals get their genes into the next generation. But even if this is so, what follows? What's consistent with the way we evolved is one thing; what's good or bad is another. Lower back pain, for example, is consistent with the way we evolved, and hence natural, since it results from our having become bipedal. Yet no one would say that lower back pain is good. Similarly, shaving, we may say, is unnatural, because we evolved to sprout hair. Yet no one would say that shaving is bad. Perhaps gay marriage is like shaving – unnatural but not bad.

Finally, we sometimes use the word "natural" to refer to a thing's proper function. For instance, when we say that it's natural for the heart to pump blood, we imply that pumping blood is the proper function of the heart. This leads us to the next argument against gay marriage – the teleological argument.

3) The teleological argument. A teleological argument consists of three steps. First, it identifies a thing's function, purpose, *raison d'être* – its *telos*, as the Greeks would say. Second, it determines how well the thing in question fulfills its *telos*. Third, depending on how well or how badly the thing fulfills its *telos*, it concludes that the thing is either good or bad. The *telos* of a knife, for instance, is to cut, so if this knife cuts well it's a good knife. The *telos* of an eye is to see, so if my eyes see poorly they're bad eyes.

Many opponents of gay marriage advance a teleological argument. The *telos* of marriage, they say, is to produce offspring. This is why people get married – to have a family. Gay and lesbian couples, however, can't reproduce, and so they can't fulfill the *telos* of marriage. For this reason, gay marriage shouldn't be allowed.

To this argument supporters of gay marriage might object that same-sex couples *can* have children – they can adopt, for example, or (if they're gay men) they can hire a surrogate mother, or (if they're lesbians) they can impregnate themselves with sperm from a sperm bank. Consequently, if the *telos* of marriage is to produce offspring, same-sex couples are fully capable of fulfilling the *telos* of marriage.

Moreover, many heterosexual couples either can't have children or choose not to have children. Should we conclude that these couples fail to fulfill the *telos* of marriage? Should we also prevent them from getting married? But perhaps the *telos* of marriage isn't – or doesn't have to be – to produce offspring. Perhaps instead the *telos* of marriage is – or can be – to express a loving commitment between partners. If this is the case, it would seem that same-sex partners can fulfill the *telos* of marriage just as well as could heterosexual partners.

4) The linguistic argument. According to some opponents of gay marriage, marriage is by definition the union of a man and a woman. Same-sex marriage is thus a contradiction in terms. There can be no same-sex marriage any more than there can be a four-sided triangle or a mother who has never had a child. Civil unions for same-sex couples might make sense, but not marriage.

The linguistic argument assumes that language is static, that the meanings of terms are forever fixed. But this assumption would seem to be false. Language constantly evolves. As a culture's beliefs, values, and practices change, so do the meanings it assigns to words. At one time, marriage was conceived as a fundamentally economic institution – by bringing two families together, it strengthened both economically. In those days, marriage had little to do with love. If the two spouses developed any affection for each other, they were lucky. These days, however, love is a more central component of marriage. Today's conception of marriage is thus quite different from conceptions of the past.

In recent years American culture has developed a greater understanding of and respect for gays and lesbians. It has become more accepting of the notion of gay rights. As American attitudes toward gays have become more liberal, so its conception of marriage is once again evolving. This evolving conception of marriage, we might argue, is a good, not a bad, thing. For now Americans are finally starting to realize the ideal of liberty and justice for all, and to recognize that human rights, as the name implies, should extend to *all* human beings, gay as well as straight.

5) The slippery slope argument. Finally, some opponents of gay marriage fear a slippery slope. Once we recognize same-sex marriage, thereby taking the first step down the slope, we won't – they argue – be able to stop there. Logically we'll be compelled to recognize other forms of marriage as well – such as polygamy and marriage to oneself. These other forms of marriage, however, are problematic. We shouldn't allow ourselves to slide all the way down the slope by accepting them. Therefore, we shouldn't recognize same-sex marriage either.

Supporters of gay marriage have two possible responses to the slippery slope argument. First, they might reply that we should recognize not only gay marriage but these other forms of marriage too. The right to liberty should extend as widely as possible. If people want to enter a polygamous marriage, or if they want to marry themselves, they should be free to do so. It's their lives to live as they please, as long as they don't hurt anyone else, and such forms of marriage don't appear to hurt anyone else.

Second, supporters of gay marriage might reply that gay marriage is importantly different from polygamy and marriage to oneself, that recognizing the one doesn't logically compel us to recognize the others. For example, unlike gay marriage, polygamy faces the problem of jealousy. In a polygamous marriage, one spouse might sense that another spouse is getting preferential treatment, thus creating feelings of resentment and animosity. By contrast, in a monogamous marriage, including a gay monogamous marriage, there is no third spouse who can get preferential treatment, and hence there are fewer grounds for jealousy between marriage partners. Thus, we may have good reason to reject polygamy but not gay marriage.

In 2004, a year after I saw my gay neighbors on TV, my wife and I moved to another part of town. I haven't seen the two men since then, so I don't know what has happened to them. But I like to imagine that they're happily married.

> *Questions for reflection: Should all fifty U.S. states be required to recognize gay marriage? Should all fifty states be required to ban gay marriage? Should each state be allowed to decide for itself whether to recognize or to ban gay marriage? Should gays and lesbians enjoy all the same rights as heterosexuals?*

Puzzle 19
Mr. Data

Mr. Data is an android on *Star Trek: The Next Generation*, a popular science fiction television series that ran from 1987 to 1994. Holding the rank of Lieutenant Commander, Data is third in command aboard the *U.S.S. Enterprise*, the flagship of the United Federation of Planets. Like human beings, he's able to solve complex problems, form friendships, and engage in sexual intercourse. Throughout the series, he strives to become ever more fully human, with mixed results. In one episode, for instance, he wants to learn how to tell jokes, but his timing is off. In another, he practices sneezing, without quite getting the hang of it. In a third, he enters a romantic relationship with a crew member of the *Enterprise*, but it falls apart because he can't make an emotional connection.

In "The Measure of a Man," an episode that originally aired on February 13, 1989, Bruce Maddox, a leading cyberneticist at Starfleet, proposes to disassemble Data so that he can learn how to create more androids like him. Data, however, rejects the proposal, because he is skeptical that Maddox will succeed in his task and be able to reassemble him. Maddox takes the case to court. The judge is Phillipa Louvois, who, having limited staff because her office is newly opened, assigns Jean-Luc Picard, captain of the *Enterprise*, to defend Data and William Riker, first officer of the *Enterprise*, to support the position of Maddox. At issue is whether Data has the same moral and legal rights as human beings, Vulcans, and other members of the United Federation of Planets, or whether he is the property of Starfleet.

As the legal hearing unfolds, several characters attempt to identify the central question that will help them resolve this issue. There are four such attempts, as follows:

1. Riker: Is Data a machine?
2. Maddox: Is Data sentient?
3. Data: Is Data a person?
4. Louvois: Does Data have a soul?

Let's take a closer look at each of these questions.

1. Is Data a machine? When Riker calls Data to the witness stand, he demonstrates with dramatic flair that Data is a machine. First, he has Data bend a rod of par-steel with a tensile strength of forty kilobars, a feat of strength no human being is capable of. Then he removes Data's left forearm for the Court's inspection. Finally, declaring that Data's "purpose is to serve human needs and interests," he flips Data's hidden off switch, causing the android to slump forward in the witness chair. Riker's argument is that, because Data is a machine, he lacks moral and legal rights. As such, he's the property of Starfleet.

In response to this argument, Picard admits that Data is a machine. Of course he's a machine, since he's an android and, by definition, any android is a machine. But as Picard points out, Riker needs to do more than demonstrate that Data is a machine, a fact that everybody already knows. In addition, he needs to explain why machines should lack moral and legal rights. Yet Riker fails to do this. According to Picard, Riker can't do this, because the fact that Data is a machine "is not relevant." It's not relevant because human beings "too are machines, just machines of a different type." In saying this, Picard raises an important point. Just as a water pump is a mechanical device for pumping water, so a human heart is a mechanical device for pumping blood. Just as Data's mechanical arms can bend a rod of par-steel, so human arms, equally mechanical, can bend a rod of silly putty. Since human beings are thus machines and since human beings have rights, it follows that a machine can have rights. Perhaps Data is one of the machines that have rights.

However, perhaps what Riker means to demonstrate is not that Data is a machine, but that he's a *mere* machine. If this is Riker's intention, his argument resembles the view of the philosopher René Descartes. According to Descartes, human beings differ from, say, clocks. A clock consists of a single substance – namely, a body that behaves in accordance with its programming and the laws of physics. Human beings, too, have bodies that behave in accordance with their programming and the laws of physics, but in addition, Descartes claims, we have minds. We are conscious, we are things that think, we are things that perceive, imagine, understand, will, and so forth. Insofar as we have bodies, we, like clocks, are machines. But whereas clocks are mere machines, we, having minds, are more, and whereas clocks, being mere machines, lack rights, we, being more, have rights. If, then, Data is like a clock, having no conscious experiences, he too would be a mere machine and have no rights.

If this is Riker's argument, it would, when stated formally, look like this:

1. Data isn't conscious.
2. If Data isn't conscious, then he doesn't have a mind.
3. <u>If Data doesn't have a mind, then he doesn't have rights.</u>
4. Therefore, Data doesn't have rights.

Since this argument is similar to the argument Maddox advances, let's turn directly to Maddox's argument.

2. Is Data sentient? Picard begins his questioning of Maddox by asking, "Is your contention that Lieutenant Commander Data is not a sentient being and therefore not entitled to all the rights reserved for all life forms within this Federation?" Maddox answers, "Data is not sentient, no." When Picard goes on to ask what he means by sentience, Maddox says, "Intelligence, self-awareness, consciousness." Fully spelled out, Maddox's argument parallels the Cartesian argument Riker may have advanced:

1. Data isn't intelligent, self-aware, and conscious.
2. If Data isn't intelligent, self-aware, and conscious, then he's not sentient.
3. <u>If Data's not sentient, then he doesn't have rights.</u>
4. Therefore, Data doesn't have rights.

To challenge this argument, Picard focuses on the first premise. When he asks whether Data is intelligent, Maddox quickly agrees, on the grounds that Data "has the ability to learn and understand, and to cope with new situations." When Picard asks whether Data is self-aware, Maddox squirms, confessing that the question is "exceedingly difficult." Yet Data seems to demonstrate self-awareness when he recognizes that he is "taking part in a legal hearing to determine my rights and status" and that at stake is his "right to choose" and "perhaps my very life." Finally, when Picard asks whether Data is conscious "in even the smallest degree," Maddox doesn't answer. Thus, by his own criteria – intelligence, self-awareness, and consciousness – Maddox doesn't know what he claims to know, that Data isn't sentient and hence doesn't have rights.

Picard could, but chooses not to, challenge the second and third premises of Maddox's argument as well. According to the second premise, to be sentient, one must be intelligent, self-aware, and conscious. Having just one or two of these characteristics, Maddox claims, isn't good enough – one must have all three. Yet this account of sentience accords poorly with the way the word is normally used. As the word is normally used, sentience is the ability to have sense experiences – that is, to experience one's internal and/or external environment, such as feeling a pang of hunger or hearing the bark of a dog. Used this way, sentience corresponds roughly to Maddox's third criterion, consciousness, but doesn't require either intelligence or self-awareness.

The third premise – that if one isn't sentient, one doesn't have rights – is likewise controversial. Consider, for instance, Terri Schiavo, who was in a persistent vegetative state from 1990 until 2005, when her feeding tube was removed and she died of dehydration. Because, from 1990 to 2005, her brain stem was still functional, she could blink and breathe and her heart could beat. But she seemed to have no awareness of anything that happened. Her eyes, for example, couldn't track moving objects and she couldn't recognize her husband or parents. Because her brain had shrunk to half its normal size, she was no longer the intelligent, self-aware person she once was, and she may not have been minimally conscious either, though some studies suggest that some patients in a persistent vegetative state are capable of feeling pain. Schiavo, therefore, was certainly not sentient in Maddox's sense of the term, and may not have been sentient in the ordinary sense either. Yet a great many people – including her parents, numerous lawmakers, and right-to-life advocates – vigorously protested the decision of the courts to allow her to die, because they believed she had rights, and would have believed she had rights whether or not she was sentient. A great many people, then, would argue that sentience isn't a prerequisite for having rights. If these people are correct, then Data, like Schiavo, could conceivably have rights even if he's not sentient.

3. Is Data a person? When Picard seeks to establish that Data is self-aware, Data identifies what he takes to be the central question that the legal hearing must answer: "Am I a person or property?" Many agree that the notion of personhood is central to the notion of rights. Much of the debate over abortion, for example, centers on the question whether a fetus is a person. Opponents of abortion commonly argue that it is a person, from which they infer that abortion violates its right to life and hence is wrong. Defenders of abortion, by contrast, commonly argue that it's not a person, from which they infer that it doesn't have a right to life, and thus abortion is permissible. Both sides, despite their considerable differences, widely accept that personhood is inextricably linked with rights. It is disappointing, then, that Data never answers the question he poses, and that Picard, Riker, Maddox, and Louvois ignore it altogether.

However, had they attempted to answer it, they would quickly have entangled themselves in controversy. For to determine whether Data is a person, they would first need to establish what a person is, and establishing this isn't as easy as might first appear. In its most obvious sense – what has been called its genetic sense – a person is nothing more than a member of the species *Homo sapiens*. In this sense, the president of the United States qualifies as a person, but dogs and dogwoods don't, and neither does Data. But it's not clear that personhood, in this genetic sense, is linked with rights. Why should possession of the DNA of the species *Homo sapiens*, a biological fact, endow one with rights? Do all members of the species *Homo sapiens* have rights? Do only members of the species *Homo sapiens* have rights? These questions do not admit of easy answers.

A more sophisticated account of personhood was developed by the philosopher Immanuel Kant. According to Kant, a person is any rational and autonomous being. To be autonomous, says Kant, is to be able to make free choices, while to be rational is to be able to solve relatively complex problems and understand basic moral concepts, such as duties and rights. Those who possess these two qualities have a dignity that mere things – eyeglasses and water bottles, for example – don't have. Eyeglasses and water bottles have only instrumental value – that is, they have value only insofar as they are useful as a means to achieving some end, such as being better able to see or quenching one's thirst. Persons, by contrast, have intrinsic value, value in and of themselves, whether or not they're useful as a means to achieving some end. Whereas things don't have rights, persons do. Whereas things can't be wronged, persons can.

If Kant's account of personhood is correct, all of the human beings who serve aboard the *Enterprise* – such as Picard and Riker – are persons and therefore have rights. The same is true of the members of alien species who serve aboard the *Enterprise*, including, for instance, Lieutenant Worf, a Klingon. Data, too, may qualify as a person, and may have rights. He's clearly rational, because he's able to solve complex problems and he understands what duties and rights are. He may also be autonomous, if the choices he makes are free rather than the strict result of his programming. Kant's account of personhood, however, may not be correct. Take, for example, babies and the severely brain-damaged. It seems obvious that they, as much as Picard and Riker, have rights. Such is the intuition that most people share. Yet, if Kant's account of personhood is correct, it's not at all obvious that they have rights, because they can't solve complex problems, they don't understand moral concepts, and much of their behavior is instinctive rather than freely chosen. Kant seems to have difficulty explaining how babies and the severely brain-damaged could have rights.

4. Does Data have a soul? When she issues her ruling, Louvois says, "We have all been dancing around the basic issue. Does Data have a soul?" She then confesses that she doesn't know the answer to her question, nor does she know whether she herself has a soul, adding that her question is "best left to saints and philosophers" and that she is "neither competent nor qualified to answer" it. Because she doesn't wish to declare Data the property of Starfleet when he might, for all she knows, have a soul, she rules in favor of Data: "But I have got to give him the freedom to explore that question himself. It is the ruling of this court that Lieutenant Commander Data has the freedom to choose."

Perhaps the reason Louvois doesn't know whether Data, or she, has a soul is that she doesn't consider what the term "soul" means. Just as different philosophers define the term "person" in different ways, so they define "soul" in different ways. Thales, the first philosopher in the Western tradition, for example, thinks of the soul as that which causes bodily motion. Thus, if someone waves hello, it is the person's soul that causes the hand to wave. From this definition, Thales infers that magnets have souls, because they attract iron filings, causing them to move. Not many philosophers accept Thales' reasoning, but, if we did, we could conclude that Data has a soul, since he's able to cause his body to move.

A much more common way that philosophers define "soul," a definition that goes at least as far back as Plato, is that it's the same thing as a mind. This is also the definition that Descartes, who uses the terms "soul" and "mind" interchangeably, gives. Descartes' views, which appear to have much in common with Riker's and Maddox's arguments, have already been discussed. So, if Louvois accepts the definition that Plato and Descartes give, she would need to ask whether Data has a mind – or, to use Maddox's terminology, whether Data is sentient or conscious. In this case, she would want carefully to consider whether the arguments that Riker and Maddox advance are persuasive. Unfortunately, in handing down her decision, she doesn't do this.

Like many other episodes of *Star Trek: The Next Generation*, "The Measure of a Man" raises important philosophical questions. The way it addresses those questions is, as one might expect from a one-hour television program, superficial, much more superficial than would satisfy a professional philosopher – and much more superficial than should satisfy anyone. Yet the episode succeeds insofar as it encourages viewers to think critically about whether only human beings have rights, or whether some forms of artificial intelligence can also have rights.

Questions for reflection: Is Data a machine? Is he sentient? Is he a person? Does he have a soul? Does he have rights? Could any form of artificial intelligence have rights?

Puzzle 20
The Cave

May 13, 1989

I sat in a cave, one of a multitude of prisoners. For dinner, as for so many other meals, we were served steak. Tendrils of steam rose from our plates like beckoning fingers. The aroma penetrated our nostrils; our mouths watered. We took a bite: the meat was so tender that it practically melted on our tongues. We groaned with pleasure. Where the meat came from we didn't know – and didn't care. We simply reveled in the flavor, the texture, the juice dribbling down our chins. We were content in our cave. It didn't occur to us to attempt escape.

I sat in a spacious banquet hall, one of a multitude of friends and family attending the wedding reception. I no longer recall the meal that was served, except that the entrée was some kind of meat – steak, perhaps. My mind wasn't on the meal, though. I was more concerned with the toast that I, as the best man, was expected to give after the meal. My younger brother – who was the groom, and a longtime Trekker – had dared me to raise my glass, give the Vulcan salute, and, in front of the onlooking crowd, say, "Live long and prosper!" Part of me was tempted, but I knew I'd chicken out. Actually, I was hoping I could find someone willing to give the toast in my place. I never felt comfortable giving toasts.

My brother had some vegan friends – they were a couple – who were sitting at the same table I was. Special care had been taken to serve them a vegan meal, but the catering service had goofed: their green beans were coated with butter. The two vegans took exception. The rights of animals, they complained, had been violated, and at their expense. They refused to eat not only the green beans but the rest of their meal as well. Some of the dinner guests grumbled. It was inappropriate, they thought, to use my brother's wedding as a platform for their animal rights agenda. The two vegans seemed to care more about animals than about the happy couple.

As far as I know, however, the episode didn't bother my brother and his bride, even though they weren't animal rights advocates. Neither did it bother me. In fact, I was delighted by the distraction. It gave me something to think about other than the impending toast. I was aware, of course, that an animal rights movement lurked out there somewhere, but I knew virtually nothing about it. Somehow, I had never studied the arguments for or against animal rights – even though I was going for a Ph.D. in Philosophy, and specialized in Ethics. Nonetheless, with a hunk of meat sitting on my plate, I thought I should say something in defense of meat.

"But at least the animals people eat have a life. If we didn't eat them, we wouldn't raise them, and if we didn't raise them, they'd never exist." This was the best I could think of. If I had known about it, I might have quoted Leslie Stephen, the father of Virginia Woolf, who made the same point I did, only more eloquently: "Of all the arguments for Vegetarianism none is so weak as the argument from humanity. The pig has a stronger interest than anyone in the demand for bacon. If all the world were Jewish, there would be no pigs at all."

My brother's vegan friends jumped all over me. They spoke at length about factory farming – the crowded conditions, the cages, the growth hormones, and on and on. Food animals, they said, were treated so inhumanely that nonexistence would be preferable to the kind of life they lived. I wasn't sure how to respond, because I knew nothing about factory farming. Where my meat came from I didn't know – and didn't care. I simply reveled in the flavor, the texture, the juice dribbling down my chin.

I was content in my cave.

Summer, 1991

A man came to visit me in the cave. He was middle-aged, slim, and wore glasses. Speaking with an Australian accent, he told me to turn around. I had spent my whole life in the cave, and, during all that time, I had never once turned around. Why should I have? Everything I needed, everything I wanted, was right in front of me. When I didn't move, the man grabbed me by my collar, lifted me to my feet, and forced me to turn around. In the distance was a bright light. The light hurt my eyes, so I covered them. The man told me about the light. He said that it was the entrance to the cave. Outside the cave was a world I knew nothing about, a world of equality, a beautiful world. I should strive to reach that world, the man said. His arguments were powerful, but, as my eyes began to adjust to the brightness, I could see that reaching the outside world would be difficult: the ascent was steep and rugged. Staying put would be so much easier. What should I do? I needed time to think.

I opened the book to Chapter One. "All Animals Are Equal," I read. All animals are equal? Was this guy serious? If this was what animal advocates believed, they must be full of baloney.

Ordinarily, I wouldn't have picked up the book. I was interested in women's rights, not animal rights. During the summer of 1991, my top priority was my Ph.D. dissertation – I was writing about feminist ethics. Ph.D. dissertations, though, don't pay the bills, so I also did some teaching, a couple of courses each semester. In the fall, I'd be teaching an introductory course in applied ethics. I'd already taught the course several times. I was growing weary of topics such as abortion, the death penalty, and euthanasia. I wanted to try something new. I flipped through the text I'd be using for the course. It had a section on animal rights. Perhaps I could teach that. The problem was that I knew next to nothing about animal rights. If I was going to teach the topic, I'd need to do some research.

I soon discovered that, in 1975, the Australian philosopher Peter Singer had written a book called *Animal Liberation*, and that this book had helped launch the modern animal movement. Fifteen years later, in 1990, Singer had written a second edition of the book. I decided to start with that.

I found the book in the school library. Every few days, I walked to the library from my apartment – a distance of a mile and a half – to read a chapter of the book. I finished the book in a couple of weeks. The first chapter of the book, titled "All Animals Are Equal," provided a philosophical rationale for the liberation of animals. To my astonishment, I found myself on the defensive.

By his claim that all animals are equal, Singer meant that the interests of a nonhuman animal have the same value as the comparable interests of a human being. Animals as well as human beings have interests. A cow, for instance, like a human being, has an interest in receiving pleasure and avoiding pain. Suppose, then, that we inflict massive suffering on a cow in order to give a human being a trifling pleasure. According to Singer, this is morally wrong, because it violates the principle of the equality of all animals. Someone who violates this principle is a speciesist. Speciesists believe that the interests of a nonhuman animal have less value than the comparable interests of a human being.

Most human beings, as Singer pointed out, are speciesists. I myself was a speciesist. But if speciesism were defensible, two statements would have to be true: 1) that human beings possess something that nonhuman animals lack, or that human beings possess more of something than nonhuman animals do, and 2) that this thing, whatever it turns out to be, increases the value of interests. If no such thing separated us from the other animals, we would have no basis for preferring our interests over theirs. Does such a thing exist?

Many have thought so. Human beings, for instance, are more intelligent. We also use language, transmit culture, and understand moral concepts such as duty, virtue, right, and wrong. There seems to be no end to the characteristics that separate us from the other animals.

However, as Singer argued, none of these characteristics increases the value of interests. Consider intelligence. A newborn baby, or a very severely brain-damaged person, is less intelligent than I am – indeed, is less intelligent than even a chimpanzee. If, then, intelligence was the characteristic that increased the value of interests, we'd be forced to conclude that the interests of a newborn baby, or of a very severely brain-damaged person, have less value than my comparable interests, or the comparable interests of a chimpanzee. This conclusion, however, is surely false. Therefore, intelligence doesn't increase the value of interests.

The same reasoning holds for the other characteristics too. Newborn babies and very severely brain-damaged people don't use language, don't transmit culture, and don't understand moral concepts. Yet their interests count as much as anyone else's comparable interests.

It appears, then, that nothing exists that only human beings possess, or that human beings possess more of than nonhuman animals do, *and* that increases the value of interests. But since no such thing exists, speciesism isn't defensible. Since speciesism isn't defensible, all animals are equal.

This argument struck me as powerful, as did other arguments that Singer advanced. But, I thought to myself, even if all animals are equal, what follows? Will I, for example, need to change my diet? If so, how? The answers to these questions were far from obvious.

I continued to read Singer's book. Chapter Three described in detail what happens on factory farms. From this chapter, I learned that everything my brother's vegan friends had said two years earlier was true. Animals raised on factory farms are treated abominably. If all animals are equal, this treatment must be highly unethical. Buying and consuming meat that comes from factory farms must likewise be unethical. But practically all of the meat I ate came from factory farms.

Thus, if Singer was right – as he seemed to be – I would need to modify my diet significantly.

I wasn't, however, eager to do so. I liked my diet the way it was – the food I ate was so tasty. Perhaps, I thought to myself, I shouldn't act hastily. Just because I couldn't find a flaw in Singer's arguments didn't mean there was no flaw. Singer's arguments were complex. I may have overlooked a flaw that was there.

I needed time to think. I wasn't yet ready to leave the cave.

July 31-August 1, 1992

I'd been thinking for more than a year. Finally, I was ready to leave the cave. But as I gazed toward the entrance, I saw not just one passage but many. Each was attractive in its way. Which one should I take? Did they all lead to the entrance? It was hard to tell, because the cave was dark. Then I realized something. Taking any of the passages was better than remaining where I was. So, hoping for the best, I picked what seemed to me the best passage. If it didn't work out, I could always try another. I climbed toward the entrance.

I lifted the sandwich, cut in half along the diagonal, to my lips and took a bite. It was simple food: half a can of tuna, a dollop of mayonnaise, and thinly sliced celery all mixed together and spread between two slices of toast. Over the years, I had eaten many such sandwiches, and I'd always enjoyed them. I had liked the flakiness of the tuna, the tang of the mayonnaise, and the crunch of the celery. But although this sandwich tasted exactly the same as all the others, something was different. I forced myself to swallow. The only reason I ate the sandwich was that I still had half a can of tuna. If I hadn't eaten the sandwich, I would have ended up throwing out the tuna, and that seemed pointless. I was happy when all that remained of the sandwich were a few crumbs of toast scattered on a plate. Never again would I eat a tuna sandwich.

I'd been thinking for more than a year. Somewhere along the way, I decided that Peter Singer was right. I had to make changes in my diet. But how far should I go? Many changes were possible, and each was attractive in its way. I seriously considered the following options:

1. Becoming a conscientious omnivore. Conscientious omnivores eat meat, eggs, and dairy, but only when these products come from animals who are reared and slaughtered humanely. Free-range chicken and cage-free eggs are acceptable; factory-farmed products are not.

2. Becoming a pescetarian. Pescetarians eat seafood but not other kinds of meat. If I became a pescetarian, I'd prefer wild-caught fish over farmed fish. I'd also eat bivalves, such as clams, because they appear to lack consciousness and the ability to feel pain. Anything that lacks consciousness doesn't have interests, and so I wouldn't need to take its interests into account when deciding what to eat.

3. Becoming a lacto-ovo vegetarian. Lacto-ovo vegetarians eat eggs and dairy but not meat of any kind, including seafood. Meat is problematic because the only way to get it is by killing an animal. If I became a lacto-ovo vegetarian, I'd try to buy eggs and dairy that came from humanely treated animals.

4. Becoming a vegan. Vegans refrain from all animal products, usually even honey. Even when we treat food animals humanely, we still use them as mere means – means to satisfy our palates – and this, according to vegans, is impermissible.

I didn't know which of these options to choose, and so for a long time I didn't choose any. Then I realized something. Choosing any of these options was better than choosing none. So, hoping for the best, I picked what seemed to me the best option. If it didn't prove satisfactory, I could always try another. On August 1, 1992, the day after I ate the tuna sandwich, I became a lacto-ovo vegetarian.

August, 1992

I stood at the entrance to the cave, peering into the outside world. The light out there was so bright that I had to shield my eyes. I could see hardly anything, only bits and pieces. I saw enough, however, to know that the man with the Australian accent had been right: the outside world was a world of equality, a beautiful world. I looked back inside the cave. In the distance, at the bottom of the cave, sat all the prisoners. They were my family and must be missing me. I needed to tell them where I'd been. As I descended into the cave, I wondered how they'd react. Would they give me their blessing? Would any of them join me?

About a week before my fall semester began, I visited my parents in Maine. That was when I broke the news that I'd become a vegetarian. My parents were surprised, but accepting. They had always accepted their children's choices in life, whatever they were. I was lucky to have understanding parents. My father even nodded approvingly and said, not once but many times, that he could easily become a vegetarian. He never did, though.

The news spread quickly to the rest of my family. They, too, were surprised, but accepting—and like my father, they declined to join me. One day, after playing a round of golf, my brother-in-law and I stopped at the clubhouse for some lunch. He ordered a burger; I had a salad, the only vegetarian option on the menu. As we ate, my brother-in-law commented, "The way animals are treated is pretty bad, but...." Then he shrugged and took another bite out of his burger. He didn't seem ready to embrace my vegetarian philosophy, and I didn't try to push it on him.

I've never tried to push vegetarianism on an unwilling audience. Doing so, I've observed, only turns people off, and turning people off does nothing to reduce the suffering of animals. As my brother's two vegan friends so clearly demonstrated, overzealousness, or the appearance of overzealousness, is counterproductive. However, when someone is willing to listen, I'm happy to share my thoughts. I'm also happy to listen, and respond, to those who disagree with me.

About the time I played the round of golf with my brother-in-law, one of my sisters and I had a spirited, but friendly, exchange of letters. My sister argued that plants as well as animals are capable of feeling pain. Thus, if it's wrong to eat animals because animals feel pain, it must for the same reason be wrong to eat plants. But if it's wrong to eat animals and it's wrong to eat plants, there's precious little left – salt comes to mind – that we *may* eat. Since we have to eat something, we may as well eat whatever we want. That includes animals.

When I asked my sister how she knew that plants can feel pain, she gave the example of the dandelion. Suppose, as I'm mowing my lawn, the blade of my lawnmower slices through the stalk of a dandelion. The yellow flower lies lifelessly on the ground. How does the plant respond? It not only grows a new flower but grows it lower to the ground, so that the next time I mow my lawn, the blade of my lawnmower slices through nothing but air. A clever plant, the dandelion! According to my sister, the dandelion grows its second flower lower to the ground in response to the pain it felt when it lost its first flower.

I objected to my sister's argument in two ways. First, I expressed doubts that dandelions, or other plants, can feel pain. For one thing, plants lack a brain or nervous system, or anything that appears to serve the same function as a brain or nervous system. For another, it makes little sense that plants would evolve with the ability to feel pain, given that they're rooted to the ground and have little opportunity to avoid painful stimuli. Imagine a fire sweeping across my lawn. The flames lick at my skin; I feel pain; I run away. But what about the dandelion? The flames lick at its leaves; it feels pain ... and then what? The plant can't run away. How cruel nature would be to endow plants with the ability to feel pain when this ability does nothing to benefit them! But didn't the ability to feel pain benefit the dandelion when I mowed my lawn? Not necessarily. Growing a second flower lower to the ground could be genetically hardwired, without the dandelion responding to pain.

Second, and more decisively, even if plants felt pain, and even if they felt pain as intensely as animals, it doesn't follow that we may as well eat animals. Suppose we're given a choice: we can eat a pound of chicken or a pound of grain. If we eat the chicken, the chicken (let's assume) will suffer; if we eat the grain, the grain (let's assume) will suffer. However, before we can eat the chicken, we must feed the chicken. To get one pound of chicken, we must feed the chicken two pounds of grain. Consequently, eating a pound of chicken will involve more suffering – that of the chicken as well as that of two pounds of grain – than will eating a pound of grain. If we wish to minimize suffering, we'd do better to be vegetarians – even on the assumption that plants can feel pain.

My sister is one of the most intelligent people I know. Yet the holes in her logic were gaping – every bit as gaping as the holes in my logic when I defended meat at my brother's wedding reception. During my years as a vegetarian, I've often observed that, when the smell of meat is in the air, logic flies out the window.

Winter, 2012

I sit at the entrance to the cave, reading Plato's Republic. *According to Plato, only what's outside the cave is real; what's inside is a mere imitation of reality. I look outside the cave, and then I look inside the cave. No. Plato got it nearly backwards. What's real is inside the cave. What's outside is a fiction, an ideal, the way things ought to be rather than the way things are. But it's a useful fiction. Ideals provide standards against which to measure the real world, and they can inspire people to make the real world better. We don't live in a world of equality. But we could. I pledge to do my best to make the cave a better place for all of us.*

Much has happened in the last two decades. More people know how food animals are raised and slaughtered, and more people have become conscientious omnivores, pescetarians, lacto-ovo vegetarians, and vegans. Even one of my brothers – not the one with the two vegan friends – turned vegetarian a couple of years ago. Today, moreover, there are more vegetarian and vegan restaurants, and many more restaurants offer at least one vegetarian option. The fake meat industry, too, has burgeoned, the quality of its products having improved markedly. In 1992, I tried products called Fakin' Bacon and Phony Baloney. I could scarcely gag them down. Those days are long gone.

The conditions in which food animals are raised and slaughtered have in some respects also gotten better. Some cages and stalls, for instance, are now larger. But there's still a long, long way to go. Battery cages, veal stalls, sow crates; beak trimming, cattle branding, tail docking; ammonia burn, mastitis, porcine stress syndrome; electrified baths, downers, desensitized or inexperienced slaughterhouse employees – these are just a few of the many problems that persist. In some respects, things have even gotten worse. For example, in 1987, about 5.3 billion chickens were slaughtered in the United States – a very large number. In more recent years, that number has climbed to around 9 billion.

I, too, have changed. In 1992, I ate cage-free eggs. They were more expensive than factory-farmed eggs, but I thought that eating them was ethically better. In this, I was right. However, ethically better doesn't mean ethically unproblematic. Some years later, I learned that even cage-free eggs raise ethical concerns, since the chickens who provide cage-free eggs, although not kept in cages, are kept in crowded sheds, and their beaks are trimmed. I considered eating free-range eggs, but those were harder to find, and even free-range eggs aren't free of ethical problems. Then a miracle occurred. One summer, I started itching ferociously. My doctor, suspecting an allergic reaction, took a sample of my blood for analysis. The results came in: I was allergic to egg whites. I couldn't have been more delighted. I gave up eggs altogether.

I now believe that the ideal diet is either vegan or nearly vegan. In practice, however, I'm not so strict. I sometimes eat dairy, especially cheese, though, when I do, I try to choose dairy that comes from cows who are treated reasonably humanely. Occasionally, a twinge of guilt tugs at me, but for the most part I think it's okay not to be fanatical about what I eat. Perhaps one day another miracle will occur, and I'll discover that I'm allergic to dairy.

For me, the important issue is not whether I should be a vegan or a lacto-ovo vegetarian – or a pescetarian or a conscientious omnivore. All of these are good choices. For me, what's important is that factory farming come to an end. Reforming it isn't enough. It's an inherently unethical practice. As much as possible, we should all refuse to purchase and consume meat, eggs, and dairy that come from factory farms.

On August 1 of this year, I'll celebrate my twentieth anniversary as a vegetarian. On that day, I'd like to dine at a vegetarian or vegan restaurant. I'll eat like a pig.

Questions for reflection: Do only human beings have rights, or do animals also have rights? What rights do animals have? Are all animals equal? Should we refuse to purchase and consume meat, eggs, and dairy that come from factory farms? Should we be vegetarians or vegans?

PART IV
Responding to Violations of Human Rights

Puzzle 21
Home Invasion

Sunday, July 22, 2007, was an ordinary day for the Petit family. William Petit, 50, an endocrinologist and expert on diabetes, played a round of golf with his father. Dr. Petit's wife, Jennifer Hawke-Petit, 48, took their eleven-year-old daughter Michaela to the local Stop and Shop to pick up the ingredients for the meal – pasta with homemade sauce and salad with balsamic vinaigrette – that Michaela, who had a passion for cooking, was going to prepare for the family. The Petits' other daughter, Hayley, aged seventeen, looked forward to attending Dartmouth College, her father's alma mater, in the fall. She planned to follow in her father's footsteps, studying medicine to become a doctor. The Petit family was well-respected and well-to-do, living in a $387,000 eight-room house on Sorghum Mill Drive in the well-to-do town of Cheshire, Connecticut.

None of the family knew that criminal eyes had spotted Mrs. Hawke-Petit and Michaela at the supermarket and followed them back to their home. None of the family knew that it had been targeted for a home invasion.

The men plotting the home invasion were Steven Hayes, 44, and Joshua Komisarjevsky, 26. Hayes and Komisarjevsky had known each other for only a few months, having met at a halfway house in Hartford. Both were on parole, and both had long criminal records.

Hayes lived with his mother and two teenage children in Winsted, Connecticut. His specialty was breaking into cars. He'd visit a park, pick out a car, and break into it by smashing one of its windows with a rock. Sometimes he'd steal the car, but more often he'd steal only some items within the car. He smoked marijuana and got high on cocaine. The first time he was arrested was at age sixteen. Over the next quarter century, he spent time in seventeen different prisons and detention centers – for auto theft, burglary, drug possession, and other crimes. But no matter how many crimes he committed, he'd sooner or later be let out on parole. The most recent crime for which he'd been arrested –

breaking into a car and stealing the pocketbook inside – occurred in 2003. Four years later, he was on parole yet again, a free man.

Komisarjevsky was born and raised in Cheshire, in a house less than two miles from Sorghum Mill Drive. His great-grandfather, a Russian opera singer, married a princess, and his grandfather was a distinguished theatrical director. Although his family was wealthy and he was home-schooled by his mother, Komisarjevsky had a troubled childhood. At age fourteen he was raped by one of the foster children his parents had taken in. That same year he broke into somebody's home for the first time. Like Hayes, he did drugs: marijuana, cocaine, and crystal methamphetamine. In 2002, just barely in his twenties, he admitted to over a dozen burglaries. The judge, who stated he was a "calculated, cold-blooded predator," sentenced him to nine years in prison plus six more years of supervised parole. Yet he was out on parole in just five years, in April 2007. For a few months, as he lived with his parents and daughter in Cheshire, he wore an electronic ankle bracelet, so that authorities could monitor his whereabouts. On July 19 the ankle bracelet was removed; four days later he was inside the Petits' home.

Hayes and Komisarjevsky, having already broken into two Cheshire homes over the weekend, were eager to move on to the Petit home. They even joked about it that Sunday. "I'm chomping at the bit to get started," Hayes texted Komisarjevsky. "Need a margarita soon." "I'm putting the kid to bed hold your horses," Komisarjevsky texted back. Hayes replied, "Dude, the horses want to get loose. LOL."

At about 3:00 a.m. on Monday, July 23, Hayes and Komisarjevsky entered the Petit home through an unlocked door. Dr. Petit was sleeping on a couch on the porch. Komisarjevsky struck him four or five times on the head with a baseball bat he'd picked up at the house, and told him to be quiet and that they only wanted money. Pointing a gun at Dr. Petit, Hayes and Komisarjevsky took the doctor into the basement, tied him up, and left him there. The two criminals then searched the first floor of the house for money, but, when little turned up, they moved to the second floor, where they found Mrs. Hawke-Petit, Hayley, and Michaela. They tied the three women in their respective bedrooms, placing pillowcases over their heads, and then resumed their search for money. Eventually they stumbled across a bankbook showing an available balance between $20,000 and $30,000, and persuaded Mrs. Hawke-Petit to withdraw $15,000 when the bank opened in the morning. In the meantime, between 4:00 and 4:30, Hayes drove to a nearby gas station and purchased $10 of gas, which he placed in cans taken from the Petit home.

Shortly before 9:30 Hayes and Mrs. Hawke-Petit arrived at the bank. Hayes waited outside while Mrs. Hawke-Petit withdrew the $15,000. As she did, she informed the teller that she and her family were being held hostage at their home, adding that Hayes and Komisarjevsky were "being nice" and that she thought they wanted only money. A bank employee called 9-1-1.

Cheshire police responded by sending officers, including SWAT team members, to set up a perimeter around the Petit home, blocking off all escape routes for Hayes and Komisarjevsky. A police helicopter was on its way. The police, hoping to take the two criminals by surprise, kept their presence undetected. By 10:00 police preparations were still underway.

While Hayes and Mrs. Hawke-Petit were at the bank, Komisarjevsky sexually assaulted Michaela, photographing the assault with his cell phone camera. When Hayes and Mrs. Hawke-Petit returned, Komisarjevsky suggested that Hayes rape Mrs. Hawke-Petit, to "square things up." As Hayes raped Mrs. Hawke-Petit on her living room floor, Komisarjevsky discovered that Dr. Petit was no longer in the basement.

When Hayes and Mrs. Hawke-Petit returned from the bank, Dr. Petit was still lying in the basement, tied to a post with his arms and legs bound. When he heard one of the perpetrators say, "Don't worry, it's going to be all over in a couple of minutes," Dr. Petit was convinced that he and his family were about to be killed. Feeling a "jolt of adrenaline," he managed to get himself loose from the post. He hopped up a set of stairs to the outside basement door, forced the door open, and then – in a stormy soaking rain – rolled his way across his backyard. He called to his neighbor, who at first didn't recognize him because the wounds he'd sustained from being struck with the baseball bat were so severe. The neighbor took Dr. Petit into his home and called 9-1-1. This happened at about 9:50.

When Komisarjevsky informed Hayes that Dr. Petit had escaped, Hayes – who was still raping Mrs. Hawke-Petit – strangled his victim to death. Then he poured some of the gasoline he'd bought earlier in the morning on her lifeless body, poured more on Hayley and Michaela, who were still alive and still tied in their bedrooms, and poured the rest throughout the house. After lighting the gasoline on fire, he and Komisarjevsky fled the scene in the Petits' SUV. By 10:01, just a block from the Petits' house, the two perpetrators ran into a police blockade and were arrested.

A blaze engulfed the Petits' house. Firefighters put it out as quickly as they could, but it was too late for Hayley and Michaela. The two girls died of smoke inhalation.

In 2009 the legislature of the State of Connecticut voted to abolish the death penalty, but Governor Jodi Rell, citing the Cheshire home invasion as a reason that the death penalty was necessary, vetoed the legislation. On December 2, 2010, Steven Hayes was sentenced to death by lethal injection; on January 27, 2012, Joshua Komisarjevsky was sentenced to death by lethal injection. Less than three months after Komisarjevsky's sentence, in April 2012, the legislature of the State of Connecticut once again voted to abolish the death penalty. This time the governor, now Dan Malloy, signed the legislation into law, making Connecticut the seventeenth U.S. state to abolish the death penalty. The legislation, however, wasn't retroactive. Thus, Hayes and Komisarjevsky remained on death row.

In August 2015 the Connecticut Supreme Court, by a 4-3 margin, supported Connecticut's abolition of the death penalty, but added that the failure to make the legislation retroactive was unconstitutional. It was unconstitutional, according to the Court, for two reasons. First, executing Hayes and Komisarjevsky, or any of the other eleven inmates on Connecticut's death row, "would violate the state constitutional prohibition against cruel and unusual punishment." Second, the death penalty, the Court argued, "no longer comports with contemporary standards of decency." Shortly after their decision was rendered, one of the four justices voting with the majority stepped down and was replaced with another justice. The Court reheard the case, but on May 26, 2016, it reaffirmed its earlier decision, this time by a 5-2 margin. As a result, Hayes and Komisarjevsky will not be executed. Instead, they'll live the rest of their lives in prison – with no chance of parole.

Questions for reflection: Is death by lethal injection an appropriate punishment for Steven Hayes and Joshua Komisarjevsky? Did the State of Connecticut do the right thing when it abolished the death penalty, or is the death penalty an appropriate response to the most serious violations of human rights?

Puzzle 22
Disobedience, Civil and Otherwise

Joan Andrews

In March 1986, Joan Andrews walked into an abortion clinic in Pensacola, Florida. Sighting a suction abortion apparatus, Andrews attempted to unplug the machine. In the process, she tipped the machine from its stand, damaging it. For this act, she was arrested and sentenced to five years in prison.

This wasn't Andrews' first arrest – she'd been arrested more than 130 times before, all for her antiabortion activities. She was associated with Operation Rescue, an antiabortion organization that in the 1980s supported civil disobedience modeled after that of Martin Luther King Jr. Like King, Operation Rescue advocated nonviolent protest; like King, Operation Rescue supported openly breaking laws it deemed unjust; like King, Operation Rescue drew inspiration from Christian teachings. Indeed, the name "Operation Rescue" derived from Proverbs 24:11 – "Rescue those who are drawn toward death, and hold back those stumbling to the slaughter."

During her trial, Andrews refused representation. She did so on the grounds that "the true defendants, the preborn children, received none and were killed without due process on the day of the Rescue attempt." She also showed no remorse for damaging the suction abortion machine, which she called a "weapon," and she wouldn't sign a statement that she would cease her antiabortion activities. When she was in jail, she rejected a mattress and blanket, choosing instead to sleep on the cement floor, and she rejected medical care, despite having an infection in the eye socket where her eye had been removed because of a melanoma. She rejected these things so as to identify with the preborn:

> The rougher it gets for us, the more we can rejoice that we are succeeding; no longer are we treated so much as the privileged born but as the discriminated against preborn. We must become aligned with them completely and totally or else the double standard separating the preborn from the rest of humanity will

never be eliminated. I don't want to be treated differently than my brother, my sister. You reject them, you reject me.

When she was released from prison, Andrews continued her antiabortion activities. She was frequently arrested, and she spent more time in prison.

Scott Roeder

In May 2009, Scott Roeder walked into the Reformation Lutheran Church in Wichita, Kansas. Sighting an usher handing out church bulletins during worship services, Roeder took out a gun and pulled the trigger. The usher was fatally wounded in the side of the head. Two people started to pursue Roeder, but gave up when he threatened to shoot them too. Roeder fled the scene in a car. Three hours later, police arrested him in Kansas City, 170 miles away. Roeder was sentenced to life in prison, initially a fifty-year sentence without parole, but this was later reduced to twenty-five years without parole. Given his age and deteriorating health, Roeder will likely die before he gets out of prison.

This wasn't Roeder's first arrest – he'd been arrested once before, in 1996. The 1996 arrest was related to Roeder's antigovernment activism. Police officers pulled over his car because, instead of having a license plate, a government requirement that Roeder thought was illegitimate, the car sported a placard that read "Sovereign Citizen." When the police officers discovered that Roeder had no driver's license, vehicle registration, or auto insurance – more illegitimate government requirements in Roeder's opinion – they searched the vehicle, finding explosives charges, a fuse cord, gunpowder, and nine-volt batteries. On that occasion, Roeder served eight months in prison, before his conviction was overturned on the grounds that the search of his car had been illegal.

Roeder was involved not only with antigovernment activism, but also with antiabortion activism. His arrest in 2009 was related to the latter. The usher he murdered was George Tiller, the medical director of Women's Health Care Services in Wichita, one of just three clinics in the country that provided late-term abortions. In Kansas, late-term abortions were prohibited except when two doctors certified that, without an abortion, the pregnant woman would suffer "substantial and irreversible impairment of a major bodily function." Tiller's clinic performed late-term abortions under these circumstances, as well as when the fetus was discovered late in the pregnancy to have a severe or fatal birth defect. Because of the controversy surrounding late-term abortions, Tiller was often the target of antiabortion activists. In June 1986, antiabortionists firebombed Tiller's clinic; in August 1993, an antiabortionist shot Tiller five times; from May 2004 until Tiller's death, the Kansas Coalition for Life held a daily vigil outside Tiller's clinic.

Condemnation of Tiller's murder was swift and widespread – even most antiabortion groups were horrified. For example, Operation Rescue, which by 2009 had abandoned lawbreaking activities in favor of legal means for preventing abortions, had this to say:

> We are shocked at this morning's disturbing news that Mr. Tiller was gunned down. Operation Rescue has worked for years through peaceful, legal means, and through the proper channels to see him brought to justice. We denounce vigilantism and the cowardly act that took place this morning. We pray for Mr. Tiller's family that they will find comfort and healing that can only be found in Jesus Christ.

Some antiabortionists, however, rejoiced. The Army of God, for example, a militant antiabortion organization, declared Scott Roeder an "American hero." Wiley Drake, the America's Independent Party candidate for vice president of the United States in 2008, said, "Would you have rejoiced when Adolf Hitler died during the war? I would have said, 'Amen! Praise the Lord! Hallelujah! I'm glad he's dead.' This man, George Tiller, was far greater in his atrocities than Adolf Hitler, so I am happy; I am glad that he is dead." Right-to-lifer Jacob Sullum wrote, "If you honestly believe abortion is the murder of helpless children, it's hard to see why using deadly force against those who carry it out is immoral, especially since the government refuses to act."

Concerns about Civil Disobedience

Suppose that we, like Joan Andrews and Scott Roeder, believe that abortion – or any other practice that is legal in the United States – is morally abhorrent, a serious violation of human rights. How far may we go to right the wrong? Must we restrict ourselves to only legal activities, as Operation Rescue has now committed itself to doing, or is breaking the law sometimes justified, as Martin Luther King Jr. maintained? If breaking the law is sometimes justified, must our lawbreaking be nonviolent? May activists ever destroy property? May activists ever take lives?

The United States has a long history of civil disobedience, stretching back to colonial times. The Boston Tea Party was an act of civil disobedience, as were many of the activities of the abolitionists, suffragists, and antisegregationists. Americans in the twenty-first century often look on these acts with approval. Where would civil rights, for example, be today had it not been for the courage of Martin Luther King Jr. and others like him? But if the civil disobedience of the past was justified, and sometimes even heroic, what about the civil disobedience of today's antiabortionists and other human rights advocates? Should we be equally approving of their activities? Here are some concerns:

1) The end cannot justify the means. The goal, or end, that Joan Andrews and Scott Roeder sought was respect for human rights, including the rights of the fetus. As a means to that end, Andrews damaged someone's property and Roeder took someone's life. One might question whether these means were consistent with the end. Damaging someone's property violates that person's right to property; taking someone's life violates that person's right to life. Violating rights as a means to achieve respect for rights seems hypocritical.

2) Activists assume what is questionable – that their moral views are the correct ones. To do what they did, Andrews and Roeder must have felt very strongly – indeed, with no doubt in their minds whatever – that abortion is nothing short of murder. Yet people who feel certain they're right often turn out to be wrong. Several centuries ago, for instance, leaders of the Catholic Church maintained with assuredness that the Earth is the center of the universe, their certainty so great that they placed the Italian astronomer Galileo Galilei under house arrest for holding an opposing view. Today, of course, we have strong reason to believe that the Catholic position was mistaken. A feeling of certainty, we know, is no guarantee of being correct. We might wonder, then, at the hubris of Andrews and Roeder, who assume that they're right about abortion and that so many others – all of the defenders of abortion, including some who have reflected carefully on abortion for years – are wrong.

3) Breaking the law sets a dangerous precedent, undermining democracy and social order. The laws of a society help maintain order. Thus, insofar as order is a good thing, laws are a good thing. This is true even if we personally disagree with some of the laws of our society – and how rare it must be for a person to agree with *all* of the laws of his or her society! Breaking laws, then, is problematic because it undermines order. It also undermines democracy in a society in which laws are passed through a democratic process. When activists such as Andrews and Roeder break laws, others may follow their example. If enough people break laws, order and democracy may be seriously impaired. So, even if Andrews' and Roeder's lawbreaking activities saved the lives of fetuses, and even if saving the lives of fetuses is a good thing, this good would have to be weighed against the bad of undermining democracy and social order.

Questions for reflection: Was Andrews' antiabortion activity justified? Was Roeder's antiabortion activity justified? May activists ever support their cause by breaking the law? May they ever damage property? May they ever kill people?

Puzzle 23
The Ticking Bomb Case

Terrorists have planted a dozen bombs in various buildings in New York City. You, who are in charge of the investigation, don't know in which buildings the bombs are located, but you know that, if you can't find them within the next eight hours, they will detonate. If that happens, the property damage will be extensive, and several hundred – maybe even several thousand – people will be killed, and hundreds or thousands more will be injured. You almost certainly won't be able to find the bombs on your own, and there is too little time to evacuate the city. However, you have in your custody a man who you have strong reason to believe is one of the terrorists behind the plot. There is a good chance that this man knows where the bombs are. You therefore use every means you can think of – trickery, threats, truth serum, etc. – to loosen the man's tongue. The man, though, says only that he knows nothing. With each passing minute, you become increasingly desperate. What else might you do to extract the information you need? You think and you think, until it occurs to you that you have one more option – a terrible option, but it might just work. The option is to torture the man – for example, by inserting needles under his fingernails. Should you go ahead with this plan? Would torture in these circumstances be justified?

In the brief time you have to mull on it, you think of several weighty objections to your plan. First, even though you're nearly a hundred percent certain that the man in your custody is one of the terrorists behind the plot, it's possible that he's not, that you've mistaken an innocent person for a dangerous criminal. Furthermore, even if the man is one of the terrorists, it's possible that he's telling the truth when he repeatedly insists that he doesn't know where the bombs are. Sometimes terrorists withhold vital information even from many members of their own group, so that, if one of these members is captured, he won't be able to reveal anything that could prevent the terrorist attack. Consequently, torturing the man in your custody might not produce any good results. You might not get the information you need, and the bombs might go off in any case. Should this occur, you'll have caused a man to suffer in vain.

Second, even if the man is one of the terrorists and even if he knows the locations of the bombs – both of which are highly likely – torturing him still might not produce any good results. Perhaps he'll stoically endure the pain, refusing to talk no matter what awful things you do to him. Or perhaps he'll talk, but, instead of telling you the truth, he'll send you on a wild goose chase, searching for the bombs in apartment buildings when in fact they're all in major retail stores. Under torture, people are liable to say anything, whether truth or fiction, whatever it takes to make the pain stop. During the European witch craze, for instance, many people were tortured into confessing that they and others were witches, that they and others had cast evil spells on people, that they and others had had sexual intercourse with the devil, and all sorts of other nonsense. You're worried that torturing the man in your custody will produce only misinformation – and that you won't be able to stop the terrorist plot.

Third, suppose that the man is one of the terrorists, that he knows the locations of the bombs, and that minutes after you insert the needles under his fingernails, he breaks down and tells you – truthfully – precisely where each bomb is. You disarm all of the bombs; you save hundreds – maybe thousands – of lives. Complete success, right? Not necessarily, you think to yourself. Possibly the terrorists who planted the bombs will learn from their mistakes. Possibly their failure this time will only motivate them to carry out an even deadlier attack in the future. Although you save hundreds – maybe thousands – of lives now, possibly somewhere down the road the terrorists will find a way to take the lives of tens of thousands. Is it worth saving a smaller number of lives now only to lose a larger number of lives later?

Finally, suppose that, as a result of torturing the man in your custody, you disarm the bombs, thereby saving hundreds or thousands of lives, and suppose further that the terrorists are never able to follow through with another, deadlier attack. But, you realize, there's still a problem – namely, the possibility of a slippery slope. If you resort to torture in this one instance, you may set a precedent. Sooner or later, whether from this group of terrorists or from someone else, there will be another threat to national security. Just as the college student who plagiarizes once finds it easier to plagiarize again, so you or others may find it easier to resort to torture a second time – and a third and a fourth. The end result could be an erosion of human rights. As you consider this objection to torture, you can't help but think of Abu Ghraib. You recall the photographs of the victims – getting punched, being forced to masturbate, being chained naked to a bedpost with underwear covering the head – and you recall the sadistic delight that Specialists Lynndie England and Charles A. Graner took as they posed in front of the victims. You worry that, if torture becomes an accepted practice, the torturers will become desensitized to the suffering of others.

But you also worry about the hundreds or thousands of lives that will be lost if those dozen bombs go off. You're not sure what the best decision is. Yet you have to make a decision. You pray that, whatever decision you make, it's the right one.

Questions for reflection: Is torture permissible in the ticking bomb case? Is it permissible in any other circumstances? Is it ever appropriate as a response to a threat to people's rights, or will it only lead to an erosion of human rights?

SOURCES AND FURTHER READING

Puzzle 1: Bad Blood
Brandt, A. M. (1978). Racism and research: The case of the Tuskegee syphilis study. *The Hastings Center Report, 8*(6), 21-29. Retrieved from https://dash.harvard.edu/bitstream/handle/1/3372911/brandt_racism.pdf?sequence=1

Clinton, B. (May 16, 1997). Presidential apology. Retrieved from https://www.cdc.gov/tuskegee/clintonp.htm

Heller, J. (July 26, 1972). Syphilis victims in U.S. study went untreated for 40 years. *The New York Times*. Retrieved from https://www.nytimes.com/1972/07/26/archives/syphilis-victims-in-us-study-went-untreated-for-40-years-syphilis.html

Regan, T. (2004). Human rights. In *Empty cages: Facing the challenge of animal rights*, pp 37-52. Rowman & Littlefield.

The Nuremberg code. (1947). Retrieved from https://history.nih.gov/research/downloads/nuremberg.pdf

Puzzle 2: The Child in the Basement
Le Guin, U. K. (1973, 2017). The ones who walk away from Omelas. Harper Perennial.

Mill, J. S. *Utilitarianism*. Any edition.

Puzzle 3: Noble Lie
Kant, I. *Groundwork for the metaphysics of morals*. Any edition.

Kant, I. On a supposed right to lie because of philanthropic concerns. Any edition.

Plato. *Republic*. Any edition.

Puzzle 4: Theme and Variations
Foot, P. (1967). The problem of abortion and the doctrine of the double effect. *Oxford Review, 5*. Retrieved from http://www2.pitt.edu/~mthompso/readings/foot.pdf

Kamm, F. M. (1989). Harming some to save others. *Philosophical Studies, 57*, 227-260.

Thomson, J. J. (1976). Killing, letting die, and the trolley problem. *The Monist, 59*, 204-217.

Unger, P. (1996). *Living high and letting die*. Oxford University Press.

Puzzle 5: Price Gouging

Crist, C. (September 17, 2004). Storm victims need protection. *Tampa Tribune*.

Jacoby, J. (August 22, 2004). Bring on the "price gougers." *Boston Globe*. Retrieved from http://archive.boston.com/news/globe/editorial_opinion/editorials/articles/2004/08/22/bring_on_the_145price_gougers146/

Sandel, M. J. (2009). *Justice: What's the right thing to do?* (pp. 3-10). Farrar, Straus and Giroux.

Sowell, T. (September 15, 2004). How "price gouging" helps Floridians. *Tampa Tribune*.

Treaster, J. B. (August 18, 2004). With storm gone, Floridians are hit with price gouging. *The New York Times*. Retrieved from https://www.nytimes.com/2004/08/18/us/hurricane-charley-economics-with-storm-gone-floridians-are-hit-with-price.html

Puzzle 6: The State of Nature

Hobbes, T. *Leviathan*. Any edition.

Locke, J. *Second treatise of government*. Any edition.

Puzzle 7: Veil of Ignorance

Rawls, J. (1971). *A theory of justice*. Harvard University Press.

Puzzle 8: Abduction, Rape, and Forced Marriage

Cole, D. (March 11, 2016). Kidnapped and raped at age 13, she's finally found justice. *National Public Radio*. Retrieved from https://www.npr.org/sections/goatsandsoda/2016/03/11/470075802/kidnapped-and-raped-at-age-13-shes-finally-found-justice

Kristof, N. D., & WuDunn, S. (2009). *Half the sky: Turning oppression into opportunity for women worldwide*, pp. 61-67. Vintage.

Puzzle 9: Lifeboat

Regina v. Dudley and Stephens. (1884). 14 Q.B.D. 273. Retrieved from https://cyber.harvard.edu/eon/ei/elabs/majesty/stephens.html

Sandel, M. J. (2009). *Justice: What's the right thing to do?* (pp. 31-33). Farrar, Straus and Giroux.

Simpson, A. W. B. (1984). *Cannibalism and the common law: The story of the tragic last voyage of the Mignonette and the strange legal proceedings to which it gave rise.* The University of Chicago Press.

Puzzle 10: Terri Schiavo

Caplan, A. L., McCartney, J. J., & Sisti, D. A. (eds.). (2006). *The case of Terri Schiavo: Ethics at the end of life.* Prometheus.

Cermenara, K., & Goodman, K. (July 28, 2005). Key events in the case of Theresa Marie Schiavo. Retrieved from http://science.jburroughs.org/mbahe/BioEthics/Articles/Schiavo Timeline.pdf

Puzzle 11: A Tale of Two Cities

Atomic Heritage Foundation, with Perkins, C., & Wargowski, D. (April 26, 2016). Hiroshima and Nagasaki bombing timeline. *Atomic Heritage Foundation.* Retrieved from https://www.atomicheritage.org/history/hiroshima-and-nagasaki-bombing-timeline

Bin Laden, O. (December 27, 2001). Interview with Usama bin Laden. In B. Rubin & J. C. Rubin (eds.), *Anti-American terrorism and the Middle East: A documentary reader* (p. 265). Oxford University Press.

History.com Editors. (June 21, 2011; updated August 6, 2019). 9/11 timeline. *History.com.* Retrieved from https://www.history.com/topics/21st-century/9-11-timeline

Truman, H. S. (August 9, 1945). Radio speech on the atomic bombing of Japan. In S. Engdahl (ed.) (2011), *The atomic bombings of Hiroshima and Nagasaki* (pp. 30-31). Greenhaven Press.

Puzzle 12: "You Are Causing Aggression to Us"

Broome, J. (2012). *Climate matters: Ethics in a warming world.* W. W. Norton & Company.

McKibben, B. (2010). *Eaarth: Making a life on a tough new planet.* St. Martin's Griffin.

NASA. (2019). Global climate change: Vital signs of the planet. Retrieved from https://climate.nasa.gov/

Singer, P. (2011). Climate change. In P. Singer, *Practical ethics*, 3rd ed., pp. 216-237. Cambridge University Press.

The World Bank. (2018). CO2 emissions (metric tons per capita). Retrieved from https://data.worldbank.org/indicator/en.atm.co2e.pc

Puzzle 13: Desecration of the Flag

Corn-Revere, R. (2005). Implementing a flag-desecration amendment to the U.S. Constitution: An end to the controversy ... or a new beginning? *First Reports, 6*(1). Retrieved from https://www.freedomforuminstitute.org/wp-content/uploads/2016/10/FirstReport.Flag_.Desecration_FINAL.pdf

Supreme Court of the United States. (1969). *Street v. New York*. Retrieved from https://www.law.cornell.edu/supremecourt/text/394/576

Supreme Court of the United States. (1971). *Radich v. New York*. Retrieved from https://www.law.cornell.edu/supremecourt/text/401/531

Supreme Court of the United States. (1974). *Smith v. Goguen*. Retrieved from https://caselaw.findlaw.com/us-supreme-court/415/566.html

Supreme Court of the United States. (1974). *Spence v. Washington*. Retrieved from https://www.law.cornell.edu/supremecourt/text/418/405

Puzzle 14: Academic Freedom

Friedersdorf, C. (February 9, 2015). Stripping a professor of tenure over a blog post. *The Atlantic*. Retrieved from https://www.theatlantic.com/education/archive/2015/02/stripping-a-professor-of-tenure-over-a-blog-post/385280/

Holz, R. C. (January 30, 2015). Letter to John McAdams. Retrieved from https://docs.google.com/file/d/0B4jS38HQ3f8dSDhNX1FQRnlpcTQ/edit?pli=1

Johnson, S. (July 6, 2018). Wisconsin Supreme Court sides with McAdams in dispute with Marquette. *Wisconsin Public Radio*. Retrieved from https://www.wpr.org/wisconsin-supreme-court-sides-mcadams-dispute-marquette

McAdams, J. (November 9, 2014). Marquette philosophy instructor: "Gay rights" can't be discussed in class since any disagreement would offend gay students. *Marquette Warrior*. Retrieved from http://mu-warrior.blogspot.com/2014/11/marquette-philosophy-instructor-gay.html

McAdams, J. (February 4, 2015). Marquette to Warrior Blogger: We're going to fire you. *Marquette Warrior*. Retrieved from http://mu-warrior.blogspot.com/2015/02/marquette-to-warrior-blogger-were-going.html

Will, G. F. (December 29, 2017). Academic freedom goes on trial. *The Washington Post.* Retrieved from https://www.washingtonpost.com/opinions/academic-freedom-goes-on-trial/2017/12/29/81cb9268-ebf6-11e7-9f92-10a2203f6c8d_story.html

Puzzle 15: Legalization of Drugs

Bennett, W. J. (September 19, 1989). A reply to Milton Friedman. *The Wall Street Journal.* Retrieved from http://docplayer.net/91488696-An-open-letter-to-bill-bennett.html

Friedman, M. (September 7, 1989). An open letter to Bill Bennett. *The Wall Street Journal.* Retrieved from http://docplayer.net/91488696-An-open-letter-to-bill-bennett.html

Mill, J. S. *On Liberty.* Any edition.

Puzzle 16: Extreme Poverty

Hardin, G. (1974). Lifeboat ethics: The case against helping the poor. *Psychology Today Magazine.*

Singer, P. (2011). Rich and poor. In P. Singer, *Practical ethics*, 3rd ed., pp. 191-215. Cambridge University Press.

Singer, P. (2009). *The life you can save: How to do your part to end world poverty.* Random House.

Puzzle 17: *Roe v. Wade*

McCorvey, N., & Thomas, G. (1997). *Won by love.* Thomas Nelson, Inc.

Prager, J. (December 28, 2017). Norma McCorvey: The woman who became Roe – and then regretted it. *Politico.* Retrieved from https://www.politico.com/magazine/story/2017/12/28/norma-mccorvey-obituary-216184

United States Supreme Court. (January 22, 1973). *Roe v. Wade.* Retrieved from https://caselaw.findlaw.com/us-supreme-court/410/113.html

Puzzle 18: Gay Marriage

Levin, M. (1984). Why homosexuality is abnormal. *The Monist, 67*(2), 251-283.

Mohr, R. D. (1989). *Gays/justice: A study of ethics, society, and law.* Columbia University Press.

Supreme Court of the United States. (2015). *Obergefell v. Hodges*. Retrieved from https://www.supremecourt.gov/opinions/14pdf/14-556_3204.pdf

Puzzle 19: Mr. Data

Descartes, R. Part V of *Discourse on the method of rightly conducting one's reason and seeking truth in the sciences*. Any edition.

Kant, I. *Groundwork for the metaphysics of morals*. Any edition.

McKirahan, R. (1994). Thales of Miletus. In R. McKirahan, *Philosophy before Socrates* (pp. 23-31). Hackett.

Plato. Book IV of the *Republic*. Any edition.

Snodgrass, M. (February 13, 1989). The measure of a man. Screenplay for *Star Trek: The Next Generation*. Retrieved from http://www.chakoteya.net/NextGen/135.htm

Puzzle 20: The Cave

Pollan, M. (2006). *The omnivore's dilemma: A natural history of four meals*. Penguin.

Singer, P. (1975, 1990, 2002, 2009). *Animal liberation*. Harper Perennial Modern Classics.

Singer, P., & Mason, J. (2006). *The ethics of what we eat: Why our food choices matter*. Rodale.

Puzzle 21: Home Invasion

Collins, D. (July 17, 2017). Cheshire, Connecticut, home invasion murders, 10 years later. *USA Today*. Retrieved from https://www.usatoday.com/story/news/2017/07/17/cheshire-connecticut-home-invasion-murders-10-years-later/483863001/

Cowan, A. L., & Stuart, C. (August 4, 2007). Suspect in Connecticut killings left long trail of lawbreaking. *The New York Times*. Retrieved from https://www.nytimes.com/2007/08/04/nyregion/04slay.html

Fernandez, N., & Cowan, A. L. (August 7, 2007). When horror came to a Connecticut family. *The New York Times*. Retrieved from https://www.nytimes.com/2007/08/07/nyregion/07slay.html

Williams, P. (August 13, 2015). Connecticut Supreme Court overturns death penalty in state. *NBC News*. Retrieved from https://www.nbcnews.com/news/us-news/connecticuts-top-court-overturns-death-penalty-state-n409256

Puzzle 22: Disobedience, Civil and Otherwise

Hendricks, M. (May 31, 2009). Tiller slaying, abortion opponents lose their moral standing. *Kansas City Star.*

Nathanson, B. (November/December 1989). Operation Rescue: Domestic terrorism or legitimate civil rights protest. *The Hastings Center Report,* 28-32.

Simon, S. (January 29, 2010). Roeder guilty of murdering abortion provider. *The Wall Street Journal.* Retrieved from https://www.wsj.com/articles/SB10001424052748703389004575033052416975506?mod=WSJ_hpp_MIDDLENexttoWhatsNewsThird

Singer, P. (2011). Civil disobedience, violence and terrorism. In P. Singer, *Practical ethics* (3rd ed.), pp. 256-275). Cambridge University Press.

Stumpe, J., & Davey, M. (May 31, 2009). Abortion doctor shot to death in Kansas church. *The New York Times.* Retrieved from https://www.nytimes.com/2009/06/01/us/01tiller.html

Puzzle 23: The Ticking Bomb Case

Dershowitz, A. M. (2003). Should the ticking bomb terrorist be tortured? A case study in how a democracy should make tragic choices. In A. M. Dershowitz, *Why terrorism works: Understanding the threat, responding to the challenge,* pp. 131-163. Yale University Press.

www.ingramcontent.com/pod-product-compliance
Lightning Source LLC
Chambersburg PA
CBHW030118100526
44591CB00009B/439